I0132572

Michael Elliott

THUS SAITH HOLLYWOOD

Using Movie Dialogue to Stimulate Spiritual Thought

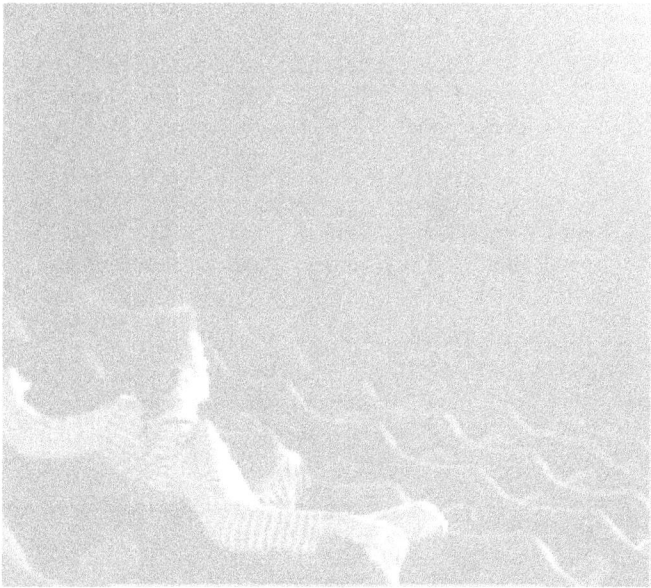

Volume One

Komeo Press

Copyright ©2011 by Michael Elliott

Published by Komeo Press
www.komeopress.com

All rights reserved. Printed in the United States of America.

No part of this book may be reproduced in any manner whatsoever
without written permission except in the case of brief quotations
embodied in critical articles and reviews.

THE HOLY BIBLE, NEW INTERNATIONAL VERSION®,
NIV® Copyright © 1973, 1978, 1984, 2011 by Biblica, Inc.™ Used
by permission. All rights reserved worldwide.

"Scripture quotations taken from the Amplified® Bible,
Copyright © 1954, 1958, 1962, 1964, 1965, 1987 by The Lockman
Foundation. Used by permission." (www.Lockman.org)

Books published by Komeo Press are available at special discounts
for bulk purchases in the United States by corporations, institutions,
and other organizations. For information contact Komeo Press at
info@komeopress.com

Text set in 12-point Garamond

ISBN-13: 978-0-9839345-0-9

To Kate, who first introduced me to this glorious new life and afterwards, to my great joy, agreed to spend the rest of it with me.

Introduction

Art has long been used to examine and comment upon the human condition. Nowhere is this more evident than in the storytelling medium of film. Whether it is a comedy, mystery, romance or action thriller, a movie, at its core, must reflect a recognizable aspect of life in order for it to effectively relate to the minds of its audience.

Because God is the Creator of life, and films must reflect life in order to be understood, we should be able to spot evidence of His handiwork woven into every film we see.

Sometimes the evidence is readily apparent, as in "Ben-Hur" or "The Prince of Egypt" which refer directly to scriptural events. Other times the inclusion is more subtle. "The Matrix" is filled with biblical references for those inclined to see them. Christian audiences flocked to theaters for "The Lord of the Rings" largely because of the spiritual symbolism to be found throughout that film.

All films will inevitably have aspects which can remind us of biblical truths or principles. Sections of scripture have been used as film titles, as in Ingmar Bergman's "Through a Glass Darkly" (1 Corinthians

13:12) or Boaz Yakin's "A Price Above Rubies" (Proverbs 31:10).

Sometimes scripture verses are woven into a character's speech as in Ren MacCormick's defense of dance in "Footloose" (Ecclesiastes 3:1-4). Other times a character's actions will mirror the events of a biblical record as in Andy Dufresne's long-suffering persistence in getting the state to provide funds for a prison library in "The Shawshank Redemption" (Luke 18:1-7).

As we make ourselves aware that God's truths have an influence that reach beyond the pews of our Sunday church services, we begin to gain the appreciation that God may very well be Hollywood's most prolific, uncredited screenwriter.

"Thus Saith Hollywood" was written as an exercise in faith. It is an attempt to connect spiritual knowledge with the most popular entertainment product in today's culture. Its purpose is not to try to change the culture in Hollywood but rather to prove that regardless of the intent of the screenwriters, directors, producers or actors, we the audience can take their product and use it to remind ourselves of the divine nature of God.

The author does not mean to imply that the films chosen for inclusion in this book are suitable for every taste or temperament. Nor does the author endorse or promote any film or screenwriter quoted here. The only aim the author has is to show how all films can remind us of the truths God would have us remember. What has guided us through this project has been our fundamental belief that, since God is everywhere present, we can find Him anywhere. We can even find Him on the screens of our neighborhood theaters.

Michael Elliott
Orlando, 2011

Michael Elliott

THUS SAITH HOLLYWOOD

The Adjustment Bureau
on
Free Will

Film: The Adjustment Bureau (2011)
Directed by: George Nolfi
Written by: George Nolfi
U.S. Distributor: Universal Pictures
Starring: Matt Damon, Emily Blunt
Rated: PG-13

About the film:
A political candidate is attracted to a young dancer only to discover that a mysterious organization is conspiring behind the scenes to keep them apart. As he learns more about this organization, he comes to the realization that there is more to the world than the eye can see.

Movie Quote:
"Free will is a gift that you'll never know how to use until you fight for it."
Harry Mitchell (Anthony Mackie) in The Adjustment Bureau (2011)

Bible Quote:
"It is for freedom that Christ has set us free. Stand firm, then, and do not let yourselves be burdened again by a yoke of slavery."
Galatians 5:1 (NIV)

Commentary:

At the core of "The Adjustment Bureau" is a false premise. It posits the idea that our free will is nothing more than illusion, given to us because we, as a race of beings, are not yet capable of living with such freedom without destroying ourselves in the process.

This, of course, is fallacy. God would not provide us with a gift without giving along with it our ability to use it effectively. Our freedom was purchased with a dear price. That price was the life of God's only begotten son. Knowing what it cost God to provide it for us, how could anyone believe He would then withhold it from us?

Our freedom is real; it is no illusion. We are free from bondage; free from fear; free from the hundreds upon thousands of doubts and worries that can multiply within us to keep us from achieving all that is within us to be.

But we are not just free from things that are negative. Our free will means that we are free to do things that are positive. We are free to act; free to love; free to serve; free to be the sons and daughters of the God who gave us our freedom in the first place. Our freedom provides us with more than the release from our spiritual chains of bondage. It also gives us the free will ability to never allow anyone or anything to ever hold us captive again. Our free will is certainly something worth fighting for. It is ours unless we willingly give it away.

Questions to consider while watching the film:
1. Why does the chairman's plan change over time? How does that equate to God's plan for the world and the lives of His people?

2. Can free will be a dangerous thing? How and why? What is the best way to protect ourselves from ourselves?

Air Force One
on
Peace

Film: Air Force One (1997)
Directed by: Wolfgang Petersen
Written by: Andrew W. Marlowe
U.S. Distributor: Columbia Pictures
Starring: Harrison Ford, Gary Oldman, Glenn Close
Rated: R

About the film:
Hijackers gain control of Air Force One and hold all occupants hostage except one. The president of the United States has managed to evade capture and must rely upon his cunning and previous military training in order to defeat his ruthless opponents and rescue his wife, child, and everyone else traveling with them.

Movie Quote:
"Peace isn't merely the absence of conflict, but the presence of justice."
President Marshall (Harrison Ford) in Air Force One (1997)

Bible Quote:
"Peace I leave with you; my peace I give you. I do not give to you as the world gives. Do not let your hearts be troubled and do not be afraid."
John 14:27 (NIV)

Commentary:

In his speech denouncing terrorism, President Marshall speaks words that resemble truth. They just do not go far enough to tell the whole story. It is true that the peace available to us through Jesus Christ does extend far beyond the absence of conflict, but it also offers us much more than the mere presence of justice.

There is a definition of peace that makes sense from a spiritual perspective. It can be said that peace is simply a state of undisturbed believing. It is a state of being where fear, doubt, and worry do not exist. Jesus Christ has given us the potential to have that kind of peace. We have the ability to believe without doubt and without reservation. He has shown us that our God is both faithful and loving. We have a God whose promises shall never fail.

Our hearts can be untroubled and we need never be afraid because we have been given the assurance that what we believe is true. Because it is true we need not be bound by doubt, worry or fear; no matter what the circumstances around us say to the contrary. The promise of peace that Jesus Christ has left us is not a promise of world peace. It is a promise that regardless of the condition of this world; regardless of the conflicts it contains; we can be assured that our God shall never leave us nor forsake us.

Questions to consider while watching the film:

1. If peace is a promise of God, why is there so much war and suffering taking place in the world?

2. What obstacles stand in the way of true God-given peace and what must we do to overcome them?

Alice in Wonderland
on
Integrity

Film: Alice in Wonderland (2010)
Directed by: Tim Burton
Written by: Linda Woolverton
U.S. Distributor: Walt Disney Studios Motion Pictures
Starring: Mia Wasikowska, Johnny Depp
Rated: PG

About the film:
Nineteen-year-old Alice once again falls down a rabbit hole and returns to that strange place known as Wonderland. She finds that the odd denizens awaiting her are filled with anticipation and the feeling that the long-overdue fulfillment of a prophecy is about to take place; a prophecy in which she is to play a major part.

Movie Quote:
"You cannot live your life to please others. The choice must be yours."
White Queen (Anne Hathaway) in Alice in Wonderland (2010)

Bible Quote:
"Am I now trying to win the approval of human beings, or of God? Or am I trying to please people? If I were still trying to please people, I would not be a servant of Christ."
Galatians 1:10 (NIV)

Commentary:

It is a natural human tendency to want to be liked. The downside is that our natural desire can and often does tempt us to present a false image of who we are or what we believe so as to gain the approval of others. The irony is rich. We might get "them" to like us, but is it really "us" that they like?

God exhorts us to walk honestly towards all men with no facades, no feigned words or false emotions. We are to simply speak and live the truth as we know it. It is not always easy. It is always profitable to God and to our souls.

There may be those who will not agree with what we say. And they may personalize the message to such an extent that they will choose to dislike the speaker as well as the speech. We cannot control how people react to us. But we can control that what we present to them is honest and true.

Besides, if we are to live our lives with the desire to please someone, we would be in a far better position if we simply focus on trying to please our God.

"Furthermore then we beseech you, brethren, and exhort you by the Lord Jesus, that as ye have received of us how ye ought to walk and to please God, so ye would abound more and more." 1 Thessalonians 4:1 (KJV)

Questions to consider while watching the film:

1. How does the Alice we see at the beginning of the film differ from the Alice at the end? What causes this change?

2. Who is the most honest character in the film? Defend your answer.

All The King's Men
on
Knowledge

Film: All The King's Men (2006)
Directed by: Steven Zaillian
Written by: Steven Zaillian
U.S. Distributor: Columbia Pictures
Starring: Sean Penn, Jude Law, Anthony Hopkins
Rated: PG-13

About the film:
Willie Stark is a down-home, grass-roots politician who capitalizes on his popularity to rise to prominence as a Louisiana governor. But what, of himself, did he lose along the way?

Movie Quote:
"To find something, anything, a great truth or a lost pair of glasses, you must first believe there will be some advantage in finding it."
Jack Burden (Jude Law) in All The King's Men (2006)

Bible Quote:
"Yea, if thou criest after knowledge, and liftest up thy voice for understanding; If thou seekest her as silver, and searchest for her as for hid treasures; Then shalt thou understand the fear of the LORD, and find the knowledge of God."
Proverbs 2:3-5 (KJV)

Commentary:

What a great truth spoken by the journalist in "All The King's Men." Too often people come to the Bible with the intent to disprove it or find fault. In reality, knowing that the scriptures contain the answers to life's eternal questions, our mindset should be one of great anticipation and excitement.

God rewards the meek and humble heart who is honestly searching for answers. The cynic has already received his "reward" and he will remain blind to the vast reservoir of truth God makes available to all who hunger for it.

Let us not forget that it is spiritual knowledge and understanding that we desire. And we desire it because it is vitally important to our lives and our growing relationship with our heavenly Father. There is one source by which this knowledge and understanding comes and He shares it only with those who love Him and share His purpose.

When we approach the Word with eager anticipation to learn something that will enrich our lives, enhance our spiritual walk, and bring us closer to God we will not have to look hard for it. God will place it on a silver platter for us to find and enjoy.

Questions to consider while watching the film:

1. Study Stark's character arc through the film. Could this story have ended differently? What choices did he make that led him down the wrong path?

2. It is said that absolute power corrupts absolutely. How does this relate to the film and how can we protect ourselves from falling into the same trap?

American Splendor
on
Limitations

Film: American Splendor (2003)
Directed by: Shari Springer Berman, Robert Pulcini
Written by: Shari Springer Berman, Robert Pulcini
U.S. Distributor: Fine Line Pictures
Starring: Paul Giamatti, Harvey Pekar, Hope Davis
Rated: R

About the film:

Harvey Pekar is a clerk at a veterans hospital who fashioned an underground comic book based upon his rather unremarkable life. He became a cult celebrity in the 1980s by illustrating his working class existence. That was just the beginning of his story.

Movie Quote:

"You might want to try believing in something bigger than yourself. It might cheer you up."
Toby (Judah Friedlander) in American Splendor (2003)

Bible Quote:

"Trust in the LORD with all your heart; and lean not unto your own understanding. In all your ways acknowledge Him, and He will make your paths straight."
Proverbs 3:5-6 (NIV)

Commentary:

As the lead character in "American Splendor" observes, "Even ordinary life gets pretty complex." How thankful should we be that there is something bigger, stronger and wiser to help guide us through the weird and wonderful maze of our lives?

Most of us are painfully aware of our limitations and shortcomings. It would be depressing to think there was nothing beyond our own experiential knowledge that we could turn to for guidance and support. Instead of depending upon something that we know is flawed (i.e., our own understanding) we can instead choose to follow a way which has been tried and found to be perfect. When we walk alone, we are weak and often confused. When we walk with spiritual awareness, we are strengthened with all the knowledge and might of the God who designed and created the world.

Adopting a humble spirit by placing our will in subjection to God's will actually frees us from carrying burdens we are too weak to bear. It relieves us of the self-imposed "responsibility" of trying to figure out a life we often do not understand. It grants us the joy and excitement of knowing that someone who is bigger than we are has something better in store for us. Life becomes simpler and much more manageable when we have God's wisdom and strength upon which to rest and rely.

Questions to consider while watching the film:

1. What was it about Harvey Pekar's life that people found interesting?

2. What is it about our lives that people might find interesting?

Amistad
on
Freedom

Film: Amistad (1997)
Directed by: Steven Spielberg
Written by: David Franzoni
U.S. Distributor: DreamWorks Distribution
Starring: Morgan Freeman, Anthony Hopkins
Rated: R

About the film:
The Amistad is a slave ship which, in 1839, saw its "cargo" revolt against their captors. Upon reaching land, the Africans are arrested and must stand trial for murder. Former U.S. president John Quincy Adams is enlisted to come to their defense.

Movie Quote:
"The natural state of mankind is instead – and I know this is a controversial idea – is freedom… is freedom. And the proof is the length to which a man, woman or child will go to regain it once taken."
John Quincy Adams (Anthony Hopkins) in Amistad (1997)

Bible Quote:
"And for you, you were dead in your transgressions and sins, in which you used to live when you followed the ways of this world and of the ruler of the kingdom of the air, the spirit who is now at work in those who are disobedient."
Ephesians 2:1-2 (NIV)

Commentary:

The opinions, as stated by John Quincy Adams in the film "Amistad," are eloquent and in their own context correct. Adams was speaking to the subject of slavery. He was addressing the morally offensive practice of men subjecting (by force) other men to bondage.

However, when speaking spiritually, the natural state of man is the opposite of freedom. Ever since the fall of Adam, man has been born into this world without the benefit of a spiritual connection to God. From the moment we take our first breath, we are legally bound to the whims of the god of this world, otherwise known as the devil.

It was for this reason that the son of God was sent to earth. What he, through his sacrifice, accomplished was to set at liberty all those who choose to accept him as Lord and believe that God raised him from the dead. He broke the chains that bound us to our spiritual adversary.

So, at the risk of disagreeing with former president John Quincy Adams, freedom is not our "natural state." It is, however, our supernatural state. It is a right dearly won for us by our savior and given to us freely by our heavenly Father.

Questions to consider while watching the film:

1. What is the scriptural definition of "slavery" and how does it apply or compare to the slavery we see in this film?

2. During the course of the film, John Quincy Adams states that the trial will be settled because "whoever tells the best story wins." What is wrong with this philosophy and how do we protect ourselves against it?

Angels & Demons
on
Science

Film: Angels & Demons (2009)
Directed by: Ron Howard
Written by: David Koepp, Akiva Goldsman
U.S. Distributor: Columbia Pictures
Starring: Tom Hanks, Ewan McGregor
Rated: PG-13

About the film:
The Vatican again turns to noted symbologist Robert
Langdon to help solve a crisis that involves four
kidnapped cardinals, a stolen container of destructive
anti-matter, and the legendary group known only as the
Illuminati. As the Vatican prepares to select its newest
pope, Langdon follows clues that are centuries old in an
attempt to rescue the four missing cardinals.

Movie Quote:
"Science and religion are not enemies. There are simply
some things that science is just too young to
understand."
Camerlengo Patrick McKenna (Ewan McGregor) in
Angels & Demons (2009)

Bible Quote:
"Do we then make void the law through faith? God
forbid: yea, we establish the law."
Romans 3:31 (KJV)

Commentary:

Throughout the years there have been those who regard scientific knowledge and religious faith to be diametrically opposed. Having such a mindset limits understanding in both categories. Science is nothing more than a systematic approach to acquiring knowledge. It is the study of the world around us using a methodology requiring observation, experimentation, and measurement. As such, science is not an enemy to faith. It is merely another means by which our faith can grow.

All of God's creation can and should be scientifically studied. God, as Creator of this world and all else, established the physical laws which govern its rule. Such laws are observable, and can be tested and measured. And, seeing as how God has been around much longer than man, it is little wonder that our science often "discovers" truths that God had already revealed to us thousands of years earlier.

One of the keys to scientific study is to share one's findings, thus enabling others to build upon the efforts of all those working in the same field. If we want to learn all there is to know about a subject, it only makes good scientific sense to include in our research, a study of the knowledge God has placed within the pages of His Word.

Questions to consider while watching the film:

1. What are some "modern day" scientific discoveries that were actually hidden in plain sight within the pages of the Bible?

2. Like science, art can also be seen as a help or a hindrance to one's faith. What are some examples of art being used for either purpose?

Apollo 13

on

Failure

Film: Apollo 13 (1995)

Directed by: Ron Howard

Written by: William Broyles Jr., Al Reinert

U.S. Distributor: Universal Pictures

Starring: Tom Hanks, Kevin Bacon, Ed Harris

Rated: PG

About the film:

When a serious malfunction occurs onboard the Apollo 13 spacecraft while on its way to the moon, a team of earthbound engineers furiously works to find a solution to bring the crew back home. Based upon an incident which took place in 1970, the film is a testament to the ingenuity and faith of a dedicated team of professionals.

Movie Quote:

"Failure is not an option."

Gene Kranz (Ed Harris) in Apollo 13 (1995)

Bible Quote:

"And it is easier for heaven and earth to pass, than one tittle of the law to fail."

Luke 16:17 (KJV)

Commentary:

While it is a wonderful mindset to have, Gene Kranz's comment cannot be construed as a statement of fact. Men fail all the time. We are fallible creatures; prone to mistakes and errors in judgment. However, in those times when failure cannot be an option, there is one way to ensure success.

God, who is infallible, has always made His will known to men. First, it was written in the stars. Later, it was handed down verbally from father to son by the patriarchs of old. Then it was committed to a written form after holy men of God spoke, being moved by holy spirit. Finally, Jesus Christ became the embodiment of God's Word in human form because he always did his Father's will and perfectly fulfilled God's law. All of these forms of truth were given to us so that we would come unto the knowledge that God has always wanted us to have.

God's Word is truth and truth can never fail. The "tittle" referred to in the quoted verse from the gospel of Luke is the tiniest part of a small letter in the Hebrew alphabet. Using this as a figurative reference, God is telling us that no part of His Word, no matter how small or seemingly inconsequential, will ever fail. Therefore, if we desire success in our lives, all we must do is trust in that Word and follow the truth it conveys to us. When failure is not an option, God's way is the only way to go.

Questions to consider while watching the film:

1. If it is true that failure does not have to be an option, why do some people, even Christians, fail?

2. How do the astronauts aboard Apollo 13 handle their fear? What can we learn from their actions?

The Apostle
on
Heaven

Film: The Apostle (1997)
Directed by: Robert Duvall
Written by: Robert Duvall
US Distribution: October Films
Starring: Robert Duvall, Farrah Fawcett
Rated: PG-13

About the film:
A preacher from Texas named Sonny Dewey decides to begin a new life, mainly because he is running from an old life that has gone bad. He lands in Louisiana, declares himself reborn as Apostle E.F. and starts afresh, preaching on the radio and restoring an old church. It is only a matter of time before the sins of his past begin to catch up with him.

Movie Quote:
"I'd rather die today and go to heaven than live to be a hundred and go to hell."
 "Sonny" Dewey (Robert Duvall) in The Apostle (1997)

Bible Quote:
"Better is one day in your courts than a thousand elsewhere: I would rather be a doorkeeper in the house of my God than dwell in the tents of the wicked."
Psalms 84:10 (KJV)

Commentary:

Sonny's declaration is a noble one. People can get so caught up in the trappings of this world that they lose their perspective. The reality is that our time on this earth is but a drop in the bucket of eternity.

While on this earth, our life will be filled with choices. There is one that is more important than all the rest combined. This one choice will determine whether we will experience the eternity that has been promised us. It is not a decision that we should put off until later.

Scripture tells us there is only one way to ensure our entrance into heaven. His name is Jesus Christ. As it says in Romans 10, when we confess him as Lord and believe that God raised him from the dead, we are saved. From that moment on, we are citizens of heaven, serving as ambassadors for Christ here on earth. Our passage to an eternity with God our Father has been secured and cannot be lost. When Christ returns a second time, he will come to gather those who will be joining him and his Father throughout all eternity.

Approximately two thousand years ago, Jesus Christ purchased a ticket to heaven for every man, woman, and child who came after him. But that ticket is not forced upon us. It needs to be claimed. Romans 10:9-10 tells us how. Simple logic should tell us when. Trying to claim a ticket after the train has left the station only ensures that we will be left behind.

Questions to consider while watching the film:

1. Is Sonny a man of God or a false preacher? Why or why not?

2. What scenes best evoke the Christian walk and mindset? Why?

Apt Pupil
on
Gifts

Film: Apt Pupil (1998)
Directed by: Bryan Singer
Written by: Brandon Boyce
U.S. Distributor: Tristar Pictures
Starring: Ian McKellan, Brad Renfro, Bruce Davison
Rated: R

About the film:
A teenage boy suspects his neighbor of being a Nazi war criminal. He confronts him but promises to keep his identity a secret if the old man would tell him stories of the atrocities that took place in the concentration camps.

Movie Quote:
"Like Icarus, we too have been given gifts: knowledge, education, experience. And with these gifts comes the responsibility of choice. We alone decide how our talents are bestowed upon the world."
Todd Bowden (Brad Renfro) in Apt Pupil (1998)

Bible Quote:
"We have different gifts, according to the grace given us. If a man's gift is prophesying, let him use it in proportion to his faith. If it is serving, let him serve; if it is teaching, let him teach."
Romans 12:6-7 (NIV)

Commentary:

Young Todd Bowden's comment is a small premonition that hints of the tragic story that will soon unfold. He may be a "gifted" individual, but he chooses to employ those gifts in pursuit of a perversely dark curiosity which results in a tragic end.

Each of us possesses certain "gifts" or "long suits." With them comes our free will choice of how to use them. Just receiving a gift does not guarantee that it will be used or used well by the one receiving it. The giver of the gift may have all the best intentions and expectations, but it is the receiver who has the ultimate decision of whether or not the gift will be put to good use.

Spiritually, God has given us the best gift of all time. We have received His gift of holy spirit. This single gift has the power to impact and affect every single thing we do or say in this world if we but choose to use it in accordance with our faith or believing.

As the giver, God's job in this particular transaction is done. We already have His gift. It is a gift that is unique and specifically designed with us in mind. All that remains is for us to make the all important choice – what are we going to do with it?

Questions to consider while watching the film:

1. Consider the film in light of 1 Corinthians 15:33. How does this scripture apply to the film's story?

2. What are some of the exhortations that God places in His Word to instruct us on how to utilize what He has given us?

Barbershop
on
Wealth

Film: Barbershop (2002)
Directed by: Tim Story
Written by: Mark Brown, Don D. Scott, Marshall Todd
U.S. Distributor: Metro-Goldwyn-Mayer
Starring: Ice Cube, Cedric the Entertainer
Rated: PG-13

About the film:
The owner of a neighborhood barbershop located in a crime-ridden section of Chicago sells out to a disreputable developer. Afterwards, he realizes that his decision will have devastating consequences to the people that view his shop as something more than just a place to get a haircut. What he does not know is how to undo the actions which he has already set into motion.

Movie Quote:
"Your daddy may not have had a whole lot of money. Oh, but he was rich, because he invested in people."
Eddie (Cedric the Entertainer) in Barbershop (2002)

Bible Quote:
"One man pretends to be rich, yet has nothing; another pretends to be poor, yet has great wealth."
Proverb 13:7 (NIV)

Commentary:

Throughout the film, Eddie offers up opinionated, politically incorrect, and raucously funny statements. They are effective because we can recognize that, at their core, they contain elements of truth. In the line quoted here, as Eddie tries to help Calvin understand what the barbershop means to their community, we can see a biblical principle at work.

When all is said and done, money is not what makes a man rich. At least money does not make a man rich in the way that really matters. All money can do is buy material things. It cannot buy character. It cannot buy respect. And as the Beatles once sang, "money can't buy you love."

These things are earned through the spending of one's self. It is an investment of a kind. It is not merely investing in other people although that is part of it. It is investing in the truth. As we plant seeds of goodness, kindness, and righteousness, we will, in due season, reap a veritable garden filled with blessings that come from God our Father.

At the end of our lives, it will not matter how much or how little we keep in our bank account. Such figures do not even appear on God's balance sheet. What makes us truly wealthy in His eyes is what we keep in our hearts.

Questions to consider while watching the film:

1. What are some of the riches that God promises to us?

2. Is being wealthy a sin? Why or why not? How are we to view the money and the possessions that we have?

Being There
on
Growth

Film: Being There (1979)
Directed by: Hal Ashby
Written by: Jerry Kosinski
U.S. Distributor: United Artists
Starring: Peter Sellers, Shirley MacLaine
Rated: PG

About the film:
A simple, middle-aged gardener, having been sheltered his entire life behind cloistered walls, is abruptly thrust into a public world he has never known. The only knowledge he has comes from his work in a garden and what he has seen on TV. Despite his innocence, he is soon mistaken for a successful and wise businessman and is courted by high-ranking politicians for his sage wisdom and advice.

Movie Quote:
"As long as the roots are not severed, all is well, and all will be well in the garden."
Chance the Gardener (Peter Sellers) in Being There (1979)

Bible Quote:
"So then, just as you received Christ Jesus as Lord, continue to live in him, rooted and built up in him, strengthened in the faith as you were taught, and overflowing with thankfulness."
Colossians 2:6-7 (NIV)

Commentary:

Even though Chance does not realize the implications of his words, the analogy that can be drawn from his comment speaks volumes to those who have spiritual ears to hear. Jesus Christ, in his parables, often used plant life as a figurative reference to how we, as spiritual beings, should grow and develop.

A plant can only be as healthy as its roots. The nutriments which cause a plant to grow are received from the earth via its root system. Cut the root and the plant will die. Spiritually, man is no different. The spiritual "garden" of our lives will flourish to the proportion that we keep ourselves rooted and grounded in the truth that can be found in Christ Jesus and the Word of God he taught.

This analogy is vividly illustrated in three of the four gospel records through the parable of the sower and the seed (Matthew 13; Mark 4; Luke 8). Of all the places that seed (representing the Word of God) landed, it produced lasting fruit only when received by the good ground (representing those who have a humble heart and receptive mind).

It is we who receive the seed of God's Word. It is we who may determine whether that seed offered to us will fall by the wayside, on stony ground, amongst thorns, or in the good ground of our hearts which allow the roots of God's Word to take hold.

Questions to consider while watching the film:

1. Why are people so inclined to view Chance as an educated and important man?

2. What is the director and screenwriter trying to say in the film's closing moments?

Cape Fear
on
The Past

Film: Cape Fear (1991)
Directed by: Martin Scorsese
Written by: Wesley Strick
U.S. Distributor: Universal Pictures
Starring: Nick Nolte, Robert De Niro
Rated: R

About the film:
Max Cady, a convicted rapist, has been released from prison after serving a fourteen year sentence. He immediately begins stalking the family of Sam Bowden, the public defender who, he believes, mishandled his case.

Movie Quote:
"If you hang onto the past you die a little each day."
Danielle (Juliette Lewis) in Cape Fear (1991)

Bible Quote:
"Brothers, I do not consider myself yet to have taken hold of it. But one thing I do: Forgetting what is behind and straining toward what is ahead, I press on toward the goal to win the prize for which God has called me heavenward in Christ Jesus."
Philippians 3:13-14 (NIV)

Commentary:

The young teenage daughter of the terrorized lawyer speaks the truth. Life, as the poets have long said, moves inexorably forward. Keeping one foot firmly planted in the place where we have already been is a sure way not to get to the place where we want to go. It is impossible to strain forward to what lies ahead if we are forever longing for that which lies behind us. We would be pulling ourselves in two opposite directions.

There is no question that our past is important. It has helped to shape us to be the men and women we are today. But our past cannot be dragged to the present. It must remain where it is if we are ever to build a future worth having. Those who live in the past have, in effect, stopped living. Life is linear, a time line upon which we all must continue to travel.

Ironically, the past in which we would prefer to stay is most likely a time when we were probably the most effective at living in the present. It is then that life is the richest. That is a lesson worth heeding. We should learn from the past. We must live in the present. Only then can we work toward the future with hope and expectation in our hearts.

Questions to consider while watching the film:

1. Did Sam Bowden act ethically in defending Max Cady? What would you have done in his place?

2. What methods does Cady use to terrorize the Bowden family? In what ways do they remind you of how the devil operates in this world?

Chariots of Fire
on
Perseverance

Film: Chariots of Fire (1981)
Directed by: Hugh Hudson
Written by: Colin Welland
U.S. Distributor: Warner Brothers
Starring: Ian Charleson, Ben Cross
Rated: PG

About the film:
Two very different runners compete in the 1924 Olympics. One is a missionary who runs for joy; the other is a man who runs to win. Together they offer the best that the United Kingdom has to offer in a global competition.

Movie Quote:
"Then where does the power come from, to see the race to its end? From within."
Eric Liddell (Ian Charleson) in Chariots of Fire (1981)

Bible Quote:
"Therefore, since we are surrounded by such a great cloud of witnesses, let us throw off everything that hinders and the sin that so easily entangles, and let us run with perseverance the race marked out for us. Let us fix our eyes on Jesus, the author and perfecter of our faith."
Hebrews 12:1-2a (NIV)

31

Commentary:

For Eric Liddell, running was a spiritual activity. He believed that the surge of power coursing through him as he ran connected him with his Creator. Not all of us will share that experience with him. However, God does use the sport in His Word to teach us other lessons.

Athletic imagery runs throughout the Bible. God continually exhorts us to endure, seeing our "race" through to the end. It is an image which aptly describes our spiritual walk.

A race has a definite beginning and end. It has boundaries or lanes within which we must stay. Many times there are obstacles in our way over which we must hurdle. But our focus is always to be on our ultimate goal. We are to keep our eyes on the finish line.

Many times during the race, we may be tempted to quit. God reminds us to look at all those who have run the race before us. We are to learn from them and draw the necessary strength and hope from their example. This will allow us to endure until the race has been completed.

And so we live our lives day by day as we would run a race, strengthening ourselves with the power of God and drawing encouragement from the believing men and women who have touched our lives with their great witness.

Questions to consider while watching the film:

1. Was Liddell right or wrong not to run on Sunday? Why or why not?

2. Who are the "witnesses" who surround us and give us encouragement to complete our race? How do they encourage us?

City of Angels
on
Believing

Film: City of Angels (1998)
Directed by: Brad Silberling
Written by: Dana Stevens
U.S. Distributor: Warner Brothers
Starring: Nicolas Cage, Meg Ryan
Rated: PG-13

About the film:
An angel falls in love with a female heart surgeon and allows her to see him. Without telling her that he is an angel, he establishes a relationship with her. As the emotions grow deeper, he knows that he has to tell her the truth. He eventually learns of a drastic measure that can be taken that will allow them to be together.

Movie Quote:
"Some things are true whether you believe in them or not."
Seth (Nicolas Cage) in City of Angels (1998)

Bible Quote:
"What if some did not have faith? Will their lack of faith nullify God's faithfulness? Not at all! Let God be true and every man a liar."
Romans 3:3-4a (NIV)

Commentary:

It is safe to say that angels probably see more disbelief than any other being. And they are probably incredulous over the difficulty humans can sometimes have believing in God's promises. Seth has the right perspective. Whether or not someone believes is not the defining element of truth.

Scripture (both the Old and the New Testaments) repeatedly testifies to the integrity of the truth God has established in His Word. He has not given man the responsibility to define what truth is. Man is called to seek the truth, study the truth, obey the truth, and believe the truth. But defining the truth is something that God has already done for us.

He has set the standard and He is faithful to honor it. Psalms 100:3 states that His truth endures to all generations. God's eternal truth will continue to exist whether men believe or not.

While there have been times in history when only a few men were faithful to believe God's Word, this fact never changed or affected the integrity and power of that Word. Yes, it is our believing that activates its power, but the potential is always present because the truth is always there.

In a world that so often disappoints, it is comforting to know that God has given us such a firm foundation upon which we may build our lives.

Questions to consider while watching the film:

1. What kind of angel is Seth and what are the characteristics that the Word uses to describe him?

2. Would you have made the choice Seth made? Why or why not?

Clean and Sober
on
Habits

Film: Clean and Sober (1988)
Directed by: Glenn Gordon Caron
Written by: Tod Carroll
U.S. Distributor: Warner Brothers
Starring: Michael Keaton, Morgan Freeman
Rated: R

About the film:
A man wakes up after a night of "hard partying." He discovers that he has a dead woman in his bed and his employer has been calling him with accusations of embezzlement. He checks himself into a drug rehab center in order to escape the law but, as time goes by, he realizes that he may have a bigger problem on his hands than he originally thought.

Movie Quote:
"The best way to break old habits is to make new ones."
Craig (Morgan Freeman) in Clean and Sober (1988)

Bible Quote:
"Do not lie to each other, since you have taken off your old self with its practices and have put on the new self, which is being renewed in knowledge in the image of its Creator."
Colossians 3:9-10 (NIV)

Commentary:

Craig, an ex-addict who now runs the rehab center, offers wise words that come from the experience of someone who knows. Nature abhors a vacuum. It is a physical law. It is especially true when it pertains to the nature of man.

Stopping a habitual act without adding something new to take its place leaves the door open for that old habit to work its way back into our behavior.

We certainly recognize this with physical habits which we try to break. Smokers who want to stop smoking will often engage in new activities to take the place of reaching for a cigarette. What is true physically is, in this case, also true spiritually.

After being born again as a new creation in Christ, we are encouraged to put off our old or "natural man" ways and habits. We do this by adopting a new way of thinking and acting. It is a way that is enhanced by spiritual knowledge. It is the way of Jesus Christ.

Armed with our new man ways, we have the capability of utterly demolishing our old man or natural man ways. The more we put into practice our renewed mind behavior, the easier and more habitual our righteous actions become. Our old man can cease to exist because we have been given a better way to live and we have chosen to follow it.

Questions to consider while watching the film:

1. What does the Bible say about drugs and alcohol? Why are they dangerous?

2. What examples in the Bible can we read that illustrate our ability to "put on" the new man? What can we learn from them?

Contact
on
Purpose

Film: Contact (1997)
Directed by: Robert Zemeckis
Written by: James V. Hart, Michael Goldenberg
U.S. Distributor: Warner Brothers
Starring: Jodie Foster, Matthew McConaughey
Rated: PG

About the film:
Ellie, as a young girl, was fascinated with the stars. She is now grown and still listens for sounds from outer space. When she finally hears a message, it garners the world's attention and attracts people from every walk of life. It does not take long for Ellie to begin feeling pushed out of the spotlight of her own discovery.

Movie Quote:
"For as long as I can remember, I've been searching for something... some reason why we're here. What are we doing here?"
Ellie Arroway (Jodie Foster) in Contact (1997)

Bible Quote:
"Now all has been heard; here is the conclusion of the matter: Fear (respect) God and keep His commandments, for this is the duty of all mankind."
Ecclesiastes 12:13 (NIV)

Commentary:

The yearning that is evident in Ellie's questions is palpable and entirely understandable. Many of us once shared that same feeling of desperate longing. And it is nothing that is new to our generation.

Throughout the ages, man has always looked for the answer to the ultimate question, "What is the reason for our existence?" Unbeknown to many, the answer we seek has been recorded for eternity within the pages of the Bible. Simply put, man was created by God because God desired a family.

Just as a new parent will make preparations in expectation of bringing a baby home, all that is around us was designed by God with us in mind. The very universe was formed so that conditions would be perfect to sustain human life on this planet.

All He has ever asked in return (indeed, all any parent should ever want) is to love and be loved in return. This is our purpose. This is the reason why we are here. We were created to love God and to allow Him to love us.

"We love Him, because He first loved us." 1 John 4:19 (KJV)

Questions to consider while watching the film:

1. What does God say about the possibility of life on other planets? What does He say is the reason for the creation of the stars and planets?

2. How has the experience changed Ellie's beliefs? Why could she not be convinced before this?

The Contender
on
Meekness

Film: The Contender (2000)
Directed by: Rod Lurie
Written by: Rod Lurie
U.S. Distributor: DreamWorks Distribution
Starring: Joan Allen, Gary Oldman, Jeff Bridges
Rated: R

About the film:
A female vice-presidential candidate is a victim of a smear campaign that has been organized by a political opponent. She refuses to confirm or deny the allegations of impropriety on the basis of principle.

Movie Quote:
"Napoleon once said, when asked to explain the lack of great statesmen in the world, that 'to get power you need to display absolute pettiness; to exercise power, you need to show true greatness.' Such pettiness and greatness are rarely found in one person."
President Evans (Jeff Bridges) in The Contender (2000)

Bible Quote:
"Who is wise and understanding among you? Let them show it by their good life, by deeds done in the humility that comes from wisdom."
James 3:13 (NIV)

Commentary:

We have not seen much improvement in the quality of statesmanship since Napoleon's day. If anything, it may have grown even worse. Today's political scene abounds in pettiness and we would be hard pressed to find an active political figure showing qualities that anyone could describe as "great."

The reason is as President Evans explains. The characteristics it takes to gain power are not the same characteristics that are needed to use that power to serve a nation or a people. Unfortunately, the self-serving position seekers often get the jobs they want but they cannot (or will not) perform those jobs in the way we the people need them to perform.

Believe it or not, the quality most needed in a successful leader is meekness or humility. It takes a strong man to stay meek when presented with such power. Most seem to succumb to the temptation to exalt themselves above those they were elected to serve.

A leader who remains meek enough to receive good and sound counsel but can also exercise the boldness to act upon that counsel for the good of the people he serves may be a rarity. But he would be a leader worthy of those who elect him.

Questions to consider while watching the film:

1. What qualities do you look for in a political candidate?

2. What motivates the various characters in the film? What informs the choices they make?

Crimson Tide
on
Ignorance

Film: Crimson Tide (1995)
Directed by: Tony Scott
Written by: Michael Schiffer
U.S. Distributor: Buena Vista Pictures
Starring: Denzel Washington, Gene Hackman
Rated: R

About the film:
Tensions run high aboard the USS Alabama, a nuclear submarine, which finds itself in the middle of an escalating conflict. Due to a possible coup in Russia, the likelihood of rebel forces gaining control of a missile site is dangerously high. Without clear orders, the captain of the sub decides to prepare for a nuclear assault upon the USSR. His second in command strongly disagrees.

Movie Quote:
"You have to set an example even in the face of stupidity."
Hunter (Denzel Washington) in Crimson Tide (1995)

Bible Quote:
"For it is God's will that by doing good you should silence the ignorant talk of foolish men."
1 Peter 2:15 (NIV)

Commentary:

The executive officer of the USS Alabama is reproving a shipmate for responding with violence to a stupid and thoughtless comment made by another sailor. He seems to know his Bible. In our lives, we will be provoked countless times by (what will appear to us to be) stupidity beyond belief.

Ignorance is anything but bliss. Dealing with it can be a frustrating and infuriating experience. When confronted with it, we are often tempted to respond in less than a loving, patient manner. We will eventually learn that there is simply no profit in our responding in such a way. Acting stupidly only fuels the fires of stupidity.

We should remember that our actions and motivations need not be dictated by outside forces. With our steps guided by love and our words framed with God's truth, we may exhibit the godly fruit of long-suffering by calmly countering ignorance with sound logic.

Light has no intellectual limits. As we act according to God's will, the spiritual light which we reflect can reach even to the darkest recesses of the human mind. The example of our lives, even in the face of stupidity, can and will have a positive impact.

Questions to consider while watching the film:

1. When faced with a direct order which goes against one's beliefs and principles, what action should be taken? Upon what do we base our decisions?

2. What procedures, outlined by God in His Word, address how to handle a disagreement among believers?

Crouching Tiger, Hidden Dragon on Faithfulness

Film: Crouching Tiger, Hidden Dragon (2000)
Directed by: Ang Lee
Written by: Hui-Ling Wang, James Schamus, Kuo Jung Tsai
US Distribution: Sony Pictures Classics
Starring: Yun-Fat Chow, Michelle Yeoh, Ziyi Zhang
Rated: PG-13

About the film:
When a legendary warrior bestows his treasured sword, The Green Destiny, to an old friend in an act that signifies his "retirement," it is stolen. The warrior and the unrequited love of his life set out together to retrieve it. They are led to the daughter of an affluent family who appears to be moonlighting as an assassin.

Movie Quote:
"A faithful heart makes wishes come true."
Lo (Chen Chang) in Crouching Tiger, Hidden Dragon (2000)

Bible Quote:
"A faithful man shall abound with blessings."
Proverbs 28:20a (KJV)

Commentary:

The word "wishes" in the quote from "Crouching Tiger, Hidden Dragon" may do more to obscure the truth than it does to help communicate it. A "wish" seems to imply a desire for something that is not promised; something that may or may not happen. It is the feeling of wanting something without having a good reason to expect anyone to give it to us. That is what a wish is. God desires something better for us.

A faithful man, such as the one in our Bible quote, shall (absolutely) abound with blessings. No wishing is involved. Instead, believing is the key to receiving those things we desire. A faithful man will set a vision for himself and then work towards that vision every day until it has been achieved.

The blessings which abound in his life are simply the fruit of his diligent actions that are faithfully performed every day. Though the faithful man works for what he wants, we can and should recognize that God is also working "behind the scenes" to reward him. God will always honor faithfulness and He faithfully rewards believing. That is not a wish. It is a promise of His Word. It is a promise that we can trust with our whole heart.

Questions to consider while watching the film:

1. What are some biblical examples of faithfulness that resulted in blessings or rewards?

2. What are some of the qualities or values that are reflected in the film's characters? How do they compare to Christian values and qualities?

Deconstructing Harry
on
Tradition

Film: Deconstructing Harry (1997)
Directed by: Woody Allen
Written by: Woody Allen
U.S. Distributor: Fine Line Features
Starring: Woody Allen, Judy Davis, Elizabeth Shue
Rated: R

About the film:
Harry Block is a novelist with writer's block who is about to receive an honorary award from the college that once expelled him. As he travels to upstate New York for the ceremony, he mentally "interacts" with characters he created and the people from his life upon which they were based.

Movie Quote:
"Tradition is the illusion of permanence."
Harry Block (Woody Allen) in Deconstructing Harry (1997)

Bible Quote:
"Jesus replied, 'And why do you break the command of God for the sake of your tradition?'"
Matthew 15:3 (NIV)

Commentary:

As with most of Woody Allen's film personas, Harry Block is a neurotic mess. But this fact does not prevent him, upon occasion, to let loose with a statement that smacks of truth. Traditions, which many people hold dear, can be an illusion and an unreliable crutch to our believing.

The worse excuse we could ever give for why we do what we do is to say that it is because we have always done it that way. That is not a healthy rationalization. It is just lazy living.

While it is true that there is a certain comfort in following traditions and rituals, there is also a downside. We should never grow so comfortable within our traditions that we refuse to respond to changing conditions or circumstances. In part, that is what happened to the Sadducees and the Pharisees of the first century AD. So intent were they on following the traditions of their fathers, they rejected the ministry of God's only begotten son which signified a changing spiritual reality.

Truth, not tradition, should be our only standard. By looking for and adhering to the truth within every situation, we can take our lives off automatic pilot and thus avoid the complacency that comes with doing something by rote.

Questions to consider while watching the film:

1. What were some traditions (or habits) that you needed to change once you became aware of the truths of God?

2. Are all traditions bad? What makes a tradition bad?

Dogma
on
Martyrdom

Film: Dogma (1999)
Directed by: Kevin Smith
Written by: Kevin Smith
U.S. Distributor: Lions Gate Films
Starring: Linda Fiorentino, Ben Affleck, Matt Damon
Rated: R

About the film:
When two angels decide to defy God's commandments and wiggle through a loophole in His law, all of humanity is threatened. It will fall upon the last known descendant of Christ to save the world. She teams up with a messenger angel named Metatron, a black apostle who was left out of the Bible because of the color of his skin, a muse turned striptease artist, and an oddball pair of humans.

Movie Quote:
"I have issues with anyone who treats faith as a burden instead of a blessing. You people don't celebrate your faith; you mourn it."
Serendipity (Salma Hayek) in Dogma (1999)

Bible Quote:
"And do not grieve the holy spirit of God, with whom you were sealed for the day of redemption."
Ephesians 4:30 (NIV)

Commentary:

It is hard to understand the logic of the stereotypical image of the downtrodden Christian. Well-intentioned Christian believers who endlessly struggle through this life with the entire weight of the world apparently upon their shoulders continue to populate the earth. To believe that we must suffer in this life to be worthy for the next is not only flawed thinking, it insults the God who sent His son to die that we might have a more abundant life.

Serendipity's comments strike home. Everything that God did, He did for us. Everything He has given us and made available to us should be the joy and rejoicing of our hearts. They are not burdens that we are being somehow forced to carry until the day we die.

Certainly we will have difficult times to endure in our lives, but that is due to the world we live in and not the God we worship. At those times, we should remember that we are designed by God to be able not only to endure the difficulties but also to triumph over them.

Manifesting the pure joy, freedom, and love that we, as believers, should feel is a far greater witness to the power of God than the sacrificial mindset of a self-appointed martyr.

Questions to consider while watching the film:

1. In the film, God is portrayed as a woman. In the Bible, God is continually given a masculine gender. Which is more accurate and why?

2. What is the relationship between angels and humans? How does it differ from the depiction in the film?

Don Juan de Marco
on
Love

Film: Don Juan de Marco (1995)
Directed by: Jeremy Leven
Written by: Jeremy Leven
U.S. Distributor: New Line Cinema
Starring: Johnny Depp, Marlon Brando
Rated: PG-13

About the film:
A young man believes himself to be Don Juan and winds up in the care of a psychiatrist. As the "greatest lover in the world" relates the story of his life and the one love that got away, the doctor discovers that the passion for his wife of thirty-four years which he had long since repressed is being rekindled.

Movie Quote:
"There are only four questions of value in life, Don Octavio. What is sacred? Of what is the spirit made? What is worth living for? And what is worth dying for? The answer to each is the same: only love."
Don Juan (Johnny Depp) in Don Juan de Marco (1995)

Bible Quote:
"And now these three remain: faith, hope and love. But the greatest of these is love."
1 Corinthians 13:13 (NIV)

Commentary:

What a great statement of truth from "Don Juan de Marco." These are words that can stir the heart even as they bring to mind the words of God that we study.

The longer we live in this world, the more we will recognize the importance of operating out of a motivation of love. Everything we do; every action we take; every decision we make; should be an extension of the love we have for God and for each other.

When we teach, we should teach not because we feel superior in knowledge, but rather because we love and wish to strengthen those to whom we can teach. When we reprove behavior, the reproof should be delivered with love and out of a desire to help the person. It should never be delivered with resentment, bitterness, or condemnation.

As the Bible tells us, love is the glue which binds all things together in harmony. The King James Version calls love the "bond of perfectness." If we wish to perfect our lives and build them to have real value in this world and in the next, we must learn to let the love of God frame our actions and guide our steps.

Questions to consider while watching the film:

1. Near the end of the film, the doctor asks his wife, "What dreams did you have that got lost along the way?" Is it important to recapture those lost dreams? Why or why not?

2. Consider the qualities of love as described in 1 Corinthians 13 and how are they illustrated in the film?

50

Doubt
on
Doubt

Film: Doubt (2008)
Directed by: John Patrick Shanley
Written by: John Patrick Shanley
U.S. Distributor: Miramax Films
Starring: Meryl Streep, Philip Seymour Hoffman
Rated: PG-13

About the film:

A strict nun suspects a parish priest of taking an improper interest in their Catholic school's newest charge: a twelve-year-old black boy. Her doubt as to the priest's morality and propriety continues to grow and feed itself as she works to remove him from his office.

Movie Quote:

"Doubt can be a bond as powerful and sustaining as certainty."
Father Brendan Flynn (Philip Seymour Hoffman) in Doubt (2008)

Bible Quote:

"Immediately Jesus reached out his hand and caught him. 'You of little faith,' he said, 'Why did you doubt?'"
Matthew 14:31 (NIV)

Commentary:

As Father Flynn asserts, doubt can be a powerful bond. It binds us to worry and, ultimately, to fear. Doubt is the first chink in the armor of our believing and, if left unresolved in our minds, it will weaken us and leave us spiritually defenseless.

Two people walked on water in the biblical record of Matthew 14. The first was Jesus. The second was Peter who had asked to join him. At first, Peter was successful. But when the winds picked up and the water began to churn, he doubted within himself the very thing he was already doing. And he began to sink.

Eliminating doubt requires us to put our trust in something larger and more powerful than our own eyes. No matter what our senses tell us; no matter what situation we are in; it is our believing or our unwavering faith that enable us to withstand and prevail.

"But when you ask, you must believe and not doubt, because the one who doubts is like a wave of the sea, blown and tossed by the wind. That person should not expect to receive anything from the Lord. Such a person is double-minded and unstable in all they do." James 1:6-8 (NIV)

Questions to consider while watching the film:

1. Was Sister Aloysius correct in the way she handled her concerns? How could she have better addressed the issue?

2. When doubt presents itself, how are we to react? What steps can we take to keep our believing strong?

The Emperor's Club
on
Stupidity

Film: The Emperor's Club (2002)
Directed by: Michael Hoffman
Written by: Neil Tolkin
US Destination: Universal Pictures
Starring: Kevin Kline, Emile Hirsch
Rated: PG-13

About the film:

A prep school teacher with idealistic beliefs and high moral principles locks horns with a new headstrong student who comes from privileged means and does not share the teacher's ethical standards.

Movie Quote:

"Aristophanes once wrote, roughly translated; 'Youth ages, immaturity is outgrown, ignorance can be educated, and drunkenness sobered, but stupid lasts forever.'"

William Hundert (Kevin Kline) in The Emperor's Club (2002)

Bible Quote:

"The fear (respect) of the LORD is the beginning of knowledge; but fools despise wisdom and discipline."

Proverbs 1:7 (NIV)

Commentary:

No one is perfect. But we all share a saving grace in that we can improve. If we have the desire and the willingness to perfect ourselves there is an unlimited amount of personal growth which we can experience and enjoy.

Not that we are able to will ourselves to grow. Our physical and our mental growth are built into our bodies. As we nourish them, the growth comes automatically. The same can be said of our spiritual lives. Just as our physical growth requires nourishment, our spiritual growth requires the nourishment of a spiritual diet that can be found through the study of God's Word.

It requires an effort on our part. When we choose not to avail ourselves of the spiritual knowledge that God has made available to all men, He describes us as being "foolish." It can be likened to the "stupidity that lasts forever" to which Aristophanes was referring.

Without the willingness to learn and the readiness to receive the nourishment of the Word, one resigns one's self to remain in a permanent state of ignorance which is a state of non-growth. Such a state of ignorance truly does last forever.

Questions to consider while watching the film:

1. God often uses plant growth as an analogy to our spiritual development. What comparisons can be made to further our understanding of how we are to grow spiritually?

2. Hundert broke his own rules at one point in the film. Why did he do this? What was the end result? Would you have done the same? Why or why not?

Enemy at the Gates
on
Envy

Film: Enemy at the Gates (2001)
Directed by: Jean-Jacques Annaud
Written by: Jean-Jacques Annaud, Alain Godard
U.S. Distributor: Paramount Pictures
Starring: Jude Law, Ed Harris, Rachel Weisz
Rated: R

About the film:
A Russian sniper is beginning to have a demoralizing effect upon the German troops during the Battle of Stalingrad. A legendary German sniper is brought in to stalk and stop him.

Movie Quote:
"But there's always something to envy. A smile, a friendship, something you don't have and want to appropriate. In this world, even a Soviet one, there will always be rich and poor."
Danilov (Joseph Fiennes) in Enemy at the Gates (2001)

Bible Quote:
"You shall not covet your neighbor's wife. You shall not set your desire on your neighbor's house or land, his manservant or maidservant, his ox or donkey, or anything that belongs to your neighbor."
Deuteronomy 5:21 (NIV)

Commentary:

The Soviet political officer Danilov paints a rather bleak picture of the human condition. The potential for envy is certainly everywhere around us but just because the potential exists does not mean that we must succumb to it.

Envy is an insidious and debilitating emotion. It is an unhealthy desire that can never be satisfied even after the object of one's desire is acquired. There will always be something bigger, or brighter, or better to envy.

When envy rules our thought life, nothing good will come as a result. Envy, as we know, causes strife and unhappiness. It can lead people to make foolish and unwise financial decisions as they try to "keep up with the Joneses."

The only way to get off of the "envy train" is to stop comparing ourselves to others. Simply being thankful for whatever we have is a far more peaceful and beneficial way to live.

"A sound heart is the life of the flesh but envy the rottenness of the bones." Proverbs 14:30 (KJV)

Questions to consider while watching the film:

1. What did Christ teach his followers about possessions? What did he believe would happen if they did not heed his teachings?

2. What are some biblical examples of envy and how did their stories end?

Evan Almighty
on
Prayer

Film: Evan Almighty (2007)
Directed by: Tom Shadyac
Written by: Steve Oedekerk
U.S. Distributor: Universal Pictures
Starring: Steve Carrell, Morgan Freeman
Rated: PG

About the film:
Newly elected congressman Evan Baxter is out to "change the world." At least that is what his campaign slogan stated. God decides to take him up on it and commands him to build an ark.

Movie Quote:
"Let me ask you something. If someone prays for patience, you think God gives them patience? Or does he give them the opportunity to be patient? If he prayed for courage, does God give him courage, or does he give him opportunities to be courageous? If someone prayed for the family to be closer, do you think God zaps them with warm fuzzy feelings, or does he give them opportunities to love each other?"
God (Morgan Freeman) in Evan Almighty (2007)

Bible Quote:
"And God is able to make all grace abound toward you; that ye, always having all sufficiency in all things, may abound to every good work."
2 Corinthians 9:8 (KJV)

MICHAEL ELLIOTT

Commentary:

The statement being made by God (played by Morgan Freeman) resounds with the sting of truth. Too many of us treat prayer as a wish list. We ask God for unattainable things as if He were Santa Claus and we were wide-eyed children lined up at the mall. What many forget is that God has already made all things available to us.

Do we desire health? God has already given it to us. (1 Peter 2:24) Be thankful, claim His promise in prayer, and believe to be healed. Do we desire wealth? God has already given it to us. (Philippians 4:19) Be thankful in prayer, claim His abundance and believe to receive it. Do we desire wisdom? God has already given it to us. (Ephesians 3:4) Claim your God-given right to study His Word and believe to grow in understanding as you pray with thanksgiving.

God does not wave His mighty hand just to do things for us. He enables us to tap into His power, His strength, His wisdom, and His knowledge so that we might do for ourselves. God does not need to give us "opportunities." There are a myriad of opportunities each day that we can seize. What he provides for us is the ability to claim that which He has already given.

Questions to consider while watching the film:

1. How does Evan deal with the unbelievers around him? Could we have done any better? What would we do differently?

2. What is prayer? How and why does it work? What are examples of effective prayers that are recorded in the Bible?

Facing the Giants
on
Impossibilities

Film: Facing the Giants (2006)
Directed by: Alex Kendrick
Written by: Alex Kendrick, Stephen Kendrick
U.S. Distributors: Destination Films; Samuel Goldwyn Films
Starring: Alex Kendrick, Shannen Fields
Rated: PG

About the film:
A losing coach with an under-performing team faces the all too real possibility of losing his job. At the end of his rope, he rededicates himself and his team to God. As he rediscovers his faith, his team discovers their untapped potential.

Movie Quote:
"We weren't supposed to have a winning season, but we do. We weren't supposed to advance to the playoffs, but we did. We're not supposed to be here, but we are."
Grant Taylor (Alex Kendrick) in Facing the Giants (2006)

Bible Quote:
"And he said, 'The things which are impossible with men are possible with God.'"
Luke 18:27 (NIV)

Commentary:

People who say, "I can't," "It's too hard," or "It's impossible," are generally proven to be right. Not because they have correctly assessed the situation but because they tend to give up before they attain their goals. Grant Taylor and his football team decide to push against the odds facing them and, as a result, share the joyous experience of exceeding everyone's expectations.

Using prayer and supplication, we are able to keep God involved in all our endeavors. This is the best ingredient for success that exists in this world. But it is not the only ingredient. We are not to sit back and simply believe for all our victories to be handed to us without effort. God expects us to do our best in all that we do. It is when our best is not enough to get the job done, that God proves to us that He is able and willing to do the rest.

Whenever we limit ourselves and our believing, whether it is due to fear, insecurity, or ignorance, we deprive ourselves of seeing the power of God prevail in our lives. We deprive ourselves of the opportunity of giving God the glory. The truth we must hold in our hearts is this: God is greater than any obstacle we face or any adversity we meet. With Him, all things truly are possible.

Questions to consider while watching the film:

1. The title suggests comparisons to David and Goliath. What similarities are there?

2. What are the figurative "giants" that must be faced by the various characters in this film?

Fight Club
on
Possessions

Film: Fight Club (1999)
Directed by: David Fincher
Written by: Jim Uhls
U.S. Distributor: 20th Century Fox
Starring: Edward Norton, Brad Pitt
Rated: R

About the film:

A disillusioned young man looking for some kind of validation to his life meets another young man who is similarly troubled. Together they initiate a "fight club" where other such men can release their aggression and frustration upon one another. Events escalate and they begin to turn their aggression outwards towards our society.

Movie Quote:

"The things you own end up owning you."
Tyler Durden (Brad Pitt) in Fight Club (1999)

Bible Quote:

"Then he said to them, 'Watch out! Be on your guard against all kinds of greed; a man's life does not consist in the abundance of his possessions.'"
Luke 12:15 (NIV)

Commentary:

Big houses, new cars, wide screen TVs, fancy computers, and designer clothes can all be seen as status symbols that, for many, mark the measure of success. What is not immediately obvious is that the cost of having such a mindset extends far beyond the mere price tag of the items.

As Tyler Durden observes, it is very easy to become slave to our possessions. The pursuit of wealth is something that has no end. He who desires to be rich can never be rich enough. There will always be newer cars, bigger houses, and more prestigious brand names to acquire. There is also the temptation to acquire "things" before we actually have the money to buy them. Debt is a deep pit into which many have fallen only to discover just how difficult it can be to find an exit.

While God desires His children to prosper, our financial prosperity should be the fruit (or result) of our labor and stewardship and not the motivation behind it. By keeping our hearts aligned with God's purpose for our lives and recognizing that He shall supply all our needs, we shall be rewarded in ways we cannot begin to imagine.

Questions to consider while watching the film:

1. What about the concept of "fight club" was so appealing to the men who participated? What were they looking for? Did they find it?

2. What does this film say about commercialism and the current state of American societal values? Do you agree with it? Why or why not?

First Knight
on
Wisdom

Film: First Knight (1995)
Directed by: Jerry Zucker
Written by: William Nicholson
U.S. Distributor: Columbia Pictures
Starring: Sean Connery, Richard Gere
Rated: PG-13

About the film:

An aging King Arthur tries valiantly to hold onto his kingdom and his new bride. The first is being threatened by a traitorous knight of his round table and the second by the virtuous new knight, Lancelot, who has fallen in love with the king's lady.

Movie Quote:

"May God grant us the wisdom to discover right; the will to choose it; and the strength to make it endure."
King Arthur (Sean Connery) in First Knight (1995)

Bible Quote:

"If any of you is lacking in wisdom, ask God, who gives to all generously and ungrudgingly, and it will be given you."
James 1:5 (NIV)

Commentary:

The prayer offered by King Arthur in "First Knight" is an indication of why his fictional kingdom of Camelot would have prospered. Anyone humbly turning to God for the answers to life's questions is sure to receive them. This is especially true if he is praying on behalf of the people who are looking to him for leadership.

What Arthur may not realize is that what he is praying for has already been granted to us. Wisdom results from acting upon the knowledge of God readily available to us in His Word. We have already been given the will to choose which course we take. It is a human right endowed by our Creator. As for strength, God gives us access to His when our own strength begins to falter. It is one of God's faithful promises to His people.

Wisdom, free will, and strength are all wonderful qualities that will lead a man or a people to victory. Arthur is already exhibiting wisdom just by praying for them. As the Bible says, "The respect of the Lord is the beginning of wisdom." It is a wise ruler who remembers this truth and acts upon it.

Questions to consider while watching the film:

1. King Arthur says early on in the film that he has learned to take the good with the bad. What does he mean by this? How does it compare to scriptural truth?

2. How is the quality of honor illustrated in the film? Which characters display examples of honor?

The Fisher King

on

The Image of God

Film: The Fisher King (1991)
Directed by: Terry Gilliam
Written by: Richard LaGravenese
U.S. Distributor: TriStar Pictures
Starring: Jeff Bridges, Robin Williams
Rated: R

About the film:
After the ramblings of Jack, a radio "shock jock," motivate one of his unbalanced listeners to commit a senseless act of violence, he finds personal redemption in trying to help one of the peripheral victims. Parry, a professor before the violent act, is now a deranged, homeless man who claims to be seeking the Holy Grail.

Movie Quote:
"I don't believe that God made man in his image."
Anne Napolitano (Mercedes Ruehl) in The Fisher King (1991)

Bible Quote:
"So God created man in His own image, in the image of God He created him; male and female He created them."
Genesis 1:27 (NIV)

MICHAEL ELLIOTT

Commentary:

Why does man have such a hard time believing what the Word of God asserts so clearly? Perhaps it is because we prefer to force an interpretation upon the Bible instead of delving more deeply into God's Word to allow it to speak for itself.

Take the scripture cited here from Genesis 1:27. For many, they interpret this verse by assuming that God looks like us. But that is not what the verse says. The verse reads that He created us in His own image. To understand the truth, we must then ask ourselves, what is the image of God?

The answer is provided in another section of the Bible. "God is spirit," John 4:24 states. Thus, the statement that we were made in God's image must be a reference to the fact that God made or created a similar spirit within man.

Further study will show that man was originally designed to be a threefold creation: body (formed from the dust of the ground); soul (made when God breathed the breath of life into Adam); and spirit (which is the very image and essence of God and our eternal link to Him).

The combination of body, soul, and spirit is what makes one a complete person. It means that we are, without question, created in the image of God.

Questions to consider while watching the film:

1. What logic does Anne use to back up her statement? How would you have responded to her?

2. How do Jack and Parry help heal each other? How does their relationship relate to God's exhortation to us?

66

Fly Away Home
on
Promises

Film: Fly Away Home (1996)
Directed by: Carrol Ballard
Written by: Robert Rodat, Vince McKewin
U.S. Distributor: Columbia Pictures
Starring: Jeff Daniels, Anna Paquin, Dana Delany
Rated: PG

About the film:

When a woman dies in an automobile accident, her thirteen-year-old daughter moves from New Zealand to Canada to stay with her estranged father. While there, she discovers a nest of goose eggs which were abandoned by their mother. She watches them hatch, bonds with the goslings, and then finds that she must be the one to teach them how to migrate south.

Movie Quote:

"Broken promises are the worst. Better not to promise anything."
Susan Barnes (Dana Delany) in Fly Away Home (1996)

Bible Quote:

"When you make a vow to God, do not delay in fulfilling it. He has no pleasure in fools; fulfill your vow. It is better not to vow than to make a vow and not fulfill it."
Ecclesiastes 5:4-5 (NIV)

MICHAEL ELLIOTT

Commentary:

We have all heard that "words are cheap." This is a popular worldly phrase that is proven untrue when examined from a spiritual perspective. Words actually come at a dear price. The words we speak have a definite impact and that impact could be either positive or negative. They can be words designed to edify and bless or they could be "fiery darts" designed to hurt and tear down.

God tells us that we shall one day appear before Him and give account for every idle word we utter (Matthew 12:36). Therefore, it would be advisable for us to think before we open our mouths. When God "speaks," the Word that is issued forth is truth. It is dependable, trustworthy, and reliable. Should we aspire to anything less?

We are told to put away lying and speak truth to every man, letting our speech be seasoned with salt (salt being a figure of speech representing commitment). Vowing a vow and keeping it is the sign of a mature, faithful person of unbroken integrity. Such a person pleases God and is deserving of respect in this world of meaningless "promises" and blatant lies.

Questions to consider while watching the film:

1. What happens when someone breaks a promise? What are the consequences that come from it?

2. Migrating geese are used as an example in management and business seminars. What spiritual lessons can we derive from observing the behavior of geese?

68

Frost/Nixon
on
Purpose

Film: Frost/Nixon (2008)
Directed by: Ron Howard
Written by: Peter Morgan
U.S. Distributor: Universal Pictures
Starring: Frank Langella, Michael Sheen
Rated: R

About the film:

Disgraced former president Richard Nixon agrees to be interviewed by TV personality David Frost in what would become a historical event. As the event draws near both participants come to realize the significance of this interview - not only for their own career or legacy but also for a nation at odds with itself.

Movie Quote:

"The unhappiest people of the world are retired – no purpose. What makes life mean something is purpose – a goal, a battle, a struggle."
Richard Nixon (Frank Langella) in Frost/Nixon (2009)

Bible Quote:

"Why, you do not even know what will happen tomorrow. What is your life? You are a mist that appears for a little while and then vanishes."
James 4:14 (KJV)

Commentary:

A life without purpose cannot be called much of a life at all. When we look back on our life as we draw near to its end, what do you suppose will provide the most satisfaction for us? Far too many of us may be surprised to find that the endeavors that took up most of our time are, in retrospect, rather insignificant.

A purpose for living provides two main benefits. First, it gives us a goal to strive for; a direction in which to follow. We need not wander aimlessly through life wondering why we are so discontent. Secondly, it provides us with a benchmark for success. With nothing to accomplish, a wasted day is merely another link to a wasted life. Having a purpose gives us something to measure, a reason to rejoice, and a life that has meaning.

Coming up with a purpose in life is no small task. Men who try to figure one out for themselves often discover too late that their self-constructed purpose for living grows into a disappointing reality, regardless of whether it is successful or not. We can be thankful that God has provided a purpose for us. He formed, made, and created us with a purpose in mind. That purpose can be found within the pages of the book which He has entrusted to us.

Questions to consider while watching the film:

1. What is man's purpose in this life that God has given us?

2. How are the qualities of ego and pride evidenced in the two central characters? What decisions do they make that are based upon them?

Grand Canyon
on
God's Word

Film: Grand Canyon (2009)
Directed by: Lawrence Kasdan
Written by: Lawrence Kasdan, Meg Kasdan
U.S. Distributor: 20th Century Fox
Starring: Danny Glover, Kevin Kline, Steve Martin
Rated: R

About the film:
On the surface, there appears to be little that an attorney, a tow truck driver, and a movie producer have in common with each other, but as events conspire to draw the characters together, we come to realize that, despite our differences, we all share in the grand adventure called life.

Movie Quote:
"All of life's riddles are answered in the movies."
Davis (Steve Martin) in Grand Canyon (1991)

Bible Quote:
"According as His divine power hath given unto us all things that pertain unto life and godliness, through the knowledge of Him that hath called us to glory and virtue."
2 Peter 1:3 (KJV)

Commentary:

With this quote, "Grand Canyon" may have stumbled upon the core principle which led to the publication of "Thus Saith Hollywood". While we cannot go as far as to say that all of life's riddles are answered in the movies, we can say with confidence that they are answered by God's Word. We can also say with confidence that, whether placed there intentionally or not, the movies of Hollywood reflect more of God's eternal truths than one might initially think.

Because screenwriters must draw from life to tell their stories, and one cannot remove or distance the Creator of life from His creation, it stands to reason that the eternal realities that God wove into the fabric of life must be present in all stories that deal with life. All it requires of us is the spiritual awareness to recognize them.

Is the movie about greed? God explains what greed is in His Word. Is it about love? No better explanation of love exists than in the Bible. The entire range or scope of human experience is handled within the Word that God has given to us. He declares that He has given us all things pertaining to life and godliness. To claim it, we simply need to go to His book. We will find the answers to the questions we seek within its pages.

Questions to consider while watching the film:

1. What does the film tell us about human relationships? How does it compare to what God tells us?

2. Who changes the most during the course of the film? Who changes the least? What caused the change or lack thereof?

The Great Buck Howard
on
Illusions

Film: The Great Buck Howard (2008)
Directed by: Sean McGinly
Written by: Sean McGinly
U.S. Distributor: Magnolia Pictures
Starring: John Malkovich, Colin Hanks, Tom Hanks
Rated: PG

About the film:
Against his father's wishes and everyone else's advice, a young man signs on as the personal assistant of an aging and demanding illusionist trying to stage a comeback to the national stage.

Movie Quote:
"Only something fake could work one hundred percent of the time."
Troy Gable (Colin Hanks) in The Great Buck Howard (2006)

Bible Quote:
"Then we will no longer be infants, tossed back and forth by the waves, and blown here and there by every wind of teaching and by the cunning and craftiness of people in their deceitful scheming."
Ephesians 4:14 (NIV)

Commentary:

Troy's skepticism is certainly understandable. After all, how many times have we been led to believe something or put our trust in someone only to discover that what we thought was true and reliable was anything but? However, just because we have been disappointed in the past does not mean that truth does not exist. It just means that we have been looking for it in the wrong places.

Buck Howard's illusions may, upon first glance, appear to be real and sometimes amazing but appearance and truth are two very different things. Deception, sleight of hand, and misdirection are all tricks of the trade for any magician or illusionist. Their acts can be very entertaining. But that is all they are.

However, there is one, capable of the greatest acts man has ever seen, who does not need to rely upon tricks and illusions. In fact, He is incapable of using them.

Our God, Creator of the heavens and the earth, cannot lie. Not even a little. Not ever. The Bible, which contains the Word that God revealed to man, is the one source we can turn to and rely upon for the truth (when read with proper spiritual discernment). It will work one hundred percent of the time without any kind of "fakery."

Questions to consider while watching the film:

1. Is it easier to believe an illusion you can see than an invisible truth? Why or why not?

2. What can we do to keep from accepting a lie or deception as truth?

The Great Debaters

on

Now

Film: The Great Debaters (2007)
Directed by: Denzel Washington
Written by: Robert Eisele
U.S. Distributor: MGM
Starring: Denzel Washington, Denzel Whitaker
Rated: PG-13

About the film:

In 1935, poet/professor Melvin Tolsen organizes and coaches a debate team for Wiley College, a small, Negro liberal arts school. Their unexpected and phenomenal success leads to an invitation to debate the national champions of Harvard University.

Movie Quote:

"The time for justice, the time for freedom, the time for equality, is always right now."
Samantha (Jurnee Smollet) in The Great Debaters (2007)

Bible Quote:

"And do this, understanding the present time. The hour has come for you to wake up from your slumber, because our salvation is nearer now than when we first believed."
Romans 13:11 (NIV)

Commentary:

The power of "now" often goes unstated and therefore unrecognized by most of us. It is gone in an instant. Fortunately for us there is always another "now" behind it to take its place. And the "now" is always overflowing with potential. Procrastination serves nobody but our spiritual adversary and delivers nothing but missed opportunities.

It is hard to understand the logic of people who make their New Year's resolutions and then count down the days until they have to start them. If there is benefit to be had by adhering to the resolution, why not start it "now?"

Every change that ever took place in our lives (be it societal, cultural, or spiritual) can be traced to that single moment in time when we decided to take action to make the change. Embracing the potential of our "now" moments is fundamental to our getting the most out of the lives we have been given. God has designed life to give us an abundant supply of "now" moments. It is up to us to use them to our benefit as well as for the benefit of those around us.

Questions to consider while watching the film:

1. What were the moments of decision in the lives of these characters? Can you spot their "now" moments and how they handled them?

2. A good debater should be able to argue either side of any issue. Why is this important? How can this lesson aid us in facing those who may disagree with our beliefs?

The Green Mile

on

Anger

Film: The Green Mile (1999)

Directed by: Frank Darabont

Written by: Frank Darabont

U.S. Distributor: Warner Brothers

Starring: Tom Hanks, Michael Clarke Duncan

Rated: R

About the film:

The guards at a Louisiana prison's death row have taken charge of a convicted murderer with a gentle heart and an unusual power to heal. They become convinced that he is innocent of the crime for which he has been sentenced to die.

Movie Quote:

"Men under strain can snap. Hurt themselves. Hurt others. That's why our job is talking, not yelling."

Paul Edgecomb (Tom Hanks) in The Green Mile (1999)

Bible Quote:

"A gentle answer turns away wrath, but a harsh word stirs up anger."

Proverbs 15:1 (NIV)

Commentary:

Paul Edgecomb, the lead jailer in the film "The Green Mile," has learned a thing or two about diffusing stressful situations. He may have learned from experience, but the same lessons can be found in the scriptures.

People who believe that the Bible is merely a book of religious platitudes are missing out on the greatest source of practical, common sense knowledge that has ever been written. God, the true author of the scriptures, designed and made man. Certainly He knows the inner workings of how man reacts and behaves in different situations.

Take the cited verse from Proverbs 15 as an example. Fighting fire with fire, in terms of dealing with anger or wrath, will only add fuel to that fire. Remaining calm and rational when provoked will help diffuse even the most volatile situations.

As we learn and apply the knowledge that God has placed in His Word, we will find that His way of doing things is really the best way to achieve the results we desire. In that regard, the Bible can be considered as the ultimate self-help book in our library.

Questions to consider while watching the film:

1. The prisoner John Coffey exemplifies the kind of attitude that Paul Edgecomb describes. Why does Coffey make the decision that he does at the end of the film?

2. The film is set on the death row of a prison. What does God's Word say about capital punishment and justice?

Hellboy
on
Darkness

Film: Hellboy (2004)
Directed by: Guillermo del Toro
Written by: Guillermo del Toro
U.S. Distributor: Columbia Pictures
Starring: Ron Perlman, Selma Blair, John Hurt
Rated: PG-13

About the film:

Rasputin intends to open a portal to hell and summon a demon that will lead the world to the apocalypse but his plans are temporarily thwarted. The baby demon was found and adopted by an expert in the paranormal who raised him to recognize right from wrong. Sixty years later, the red devil is now the world's dominant force fighting against evil.

Movie Quote:

"In the absence of light, darkness prevails."
Professor Bloom (John Hurt) in Hellboy (2004)

Bible Quote:

"Do not be yoked together with unbelievers. For what do righteousness and wickedness have in common? Or what fellowship can light have with darkness?"
2 Corinthians 6:14 (NIV)

Commentary:

The key to recognizing the truth of Professor Bloom's quote from "Hellboy" is to know that God is light. In the absence of God, darkness or evil truly will prevail. The only force more powerful than the evil that exists in this world is the truth of God that dwells in our hearts. We never want to abandon that truth.

Darkness can be suffocating. Those who have ever gone spelunking or caving and, while in the bowels of the earth, decided to turn off their flashlights experientially know the truth of that statement. But the minute the flashlight is turned back on, the darkness is gone. Light is always more powerful than the darkness. It is only the absence of light that allows darkness to exist.

So it is with spiritual light and darkness. When God's light is not present (indicating that we have turned away from Him and His Word), darkness will prevail in our lives. But the moment spiritual light manifests itself through our decision to turn to God and His will, the darkness must flee. It cannot co-exist with light.

The lesson for us is to stay within the light of God's Word. His illuminating truth enables and empowers us so that we need not descend into the darkness and the many pitfalls that await us there.

Questions to consider while watching the film:

1. The movie's main thematic question resolves around choice. Do demons have a choice?

2. The characters place a great deal of emphasis on the power contained in religious relics. Is there validity in this? Why or why not?

High Fidelity
on
Decisions

Film: High Fidelity (2000)
Directed by: Stephen Frears
Written by: D.V. DeVincentis, Steve Pink, John Cusack, Scott Rosenberg
U.S. Distributor: Buena Vista Pictures
Starring: John Cusack, Iben Hjejle, Jack Black
Rated: R

About the film:
A thirty-something record store owner is told by his girlfriend that she is leaving him due to his inability to grow and develop as a person. He makes a list of the worst five break-ups in his dating history and then decides to revisit these women to see if he can learn something about himself in the process.

Movie Quote:
"I guess it made more sense to commit to nothing, keep my options open. And that's suicide... by tiny, tiny increments."
Rob Gordon (John Cusack) in High Fidelity (2000)

Bible Quote:
"[For being as he is] a man of two minds (hesitating, dubious, irresolute), [he is] unstable and unreliable and uncertain about everything [he thinks, feels, decides]."
James 1:8 (Amplified)

Commentary:

Rob Gordon has reached an age that will resonate with many of us. It is an age where we begin to reflect upon the choices that we have made in the past with the realization that it was those choices that determined our present state of being. Rob's biggest error was in putting off making any choice that would give his life a meaningful direction.

An uncommitted man lives as a mere shadow. His life proves to be shallow and unrewarding. It is the commitments we make during our lifetimes that define who we are as individuals and what impact our lives shall have upon others.

While there is nothing wrong with keeping one's options open or staying flexible, so we might respond to new opportunities, this should not be interpreted to mean that we should never choose a course of action. We choose and, as circumstances change, we have the God-given ability to adjust our heading accordingly.

God did not give us free will in order to watch us wallow in a continual state of indecision. He wants us to set our hearts on the goals we desire and pursue those goals with vigor, energy and a fully committed mind. As we do, we will find that we are embracing life to the fullest.

Questions to consider while watching the film:

1. Do you know anyone like the employees of Rob's store? What motivates or drives them? How is Rob different?

2. What scriptures has God given us that speak to the issue of maturing and developing as we grow? How do they relate to this film?

Hitch
on
Behavior

Film: Hitch (2005)
Directed by: Andy Tennant
Written by: Kevin Bisch
U.S. Distributor: Columbia Pictures
Starring: Will Smith, Kevin James, Eva Mendes
Rated: PG-13

About the film:
The "date doctor," who has helped countless men woo the ladies of their dreams, has problems taking his own advice. Even as he helps his latest client win a seemingly unattainable girl, he runs into trouble when he decides to pursue an attractive journalist.

Movie Quote:
"Ninety percent of what you're saying isn't coming out of your mouth."
Hitch (Will Smith) in Hitch (2006)

Bible Quote:
"Because our gospel came to you not simply with words, but also with power, with the holy spirit and deep conviction. You know how we lived among you for your sake."
1 Thessalonians 1:5 (NIV)

Commentary:

When the "date doctor" gives wise counsel to his client he is, in essence, restating something the Apostle Paul once explained to the believers of Thessalonica. As the saying goes, "talk is cheap." Unfortunately, the cost of listening to and following "cheap talk" can be very dear indeed.

Eloquence is not, nor has it ever been, a reflection of character. The quality of a man is best judged by his actions, not his words. Pick just about any prominent spokesman who may have become embroiled in an ethical or moral scandal and try to reconcile the things he or she publicly said with the things he or she privately did. Which paints a more accurate picture of the person?

How a man conducts himself (publicly, privately, in any situation) speaks far more loudly than a thousand speeches on the subject. When Christ called us to be "lights in this world," he challenged us to live in this world according to his teachings and not just to give lip service to them. If we do as he exhorts, even if we never say a word, the world will recognize the Christ in us and take notice.

Questions to consider while watching the film:

1. How do you view the "service" Hitch provides to the men who hire him? Is it a form of deception as some characters claim? Why or why not?

2. What is the main lesson we, as Christians, can draw from the film as we go through the dating process?

Independence Day
on
Unity

Film: Independence Day (1996)
Directed by: Roland Emmerich
Written by: Dean Devlin, Roland Emmerich
U.S. Distributor: 20th Century Fox
Starring: Bill Pullman, Will Smith, Jeff Goldblum
Rated: PG-13

About the film:
When aliens arrive with hostile intentions, the human race must band together to defeat them or face total annihilation. The U.S. President, a cable technician, a crop duster, and a fighter pilot combine to embark on a desperate mission to save the world.

Movie Quote:
"Mankind. That word should have new meaning for all of us today. We can't be consumed by our petty differences anymore. We will be united in our common interest."
President Thomas Whitmore (Bill Pullman) in Independence Day (1996)

Bible Quote:
"Then make my joy complete by being like-minded, having the same love, being one in spirit and purpose."
Philippians 2:2 (NIV)

Commentary:

President Whitmore's address may be an idealized sentiment. But that does not mean that we should not try to live up to it. It is exactly the type of mindset that God wants us to adopt.

In times of crises, we tend to remember this exhortation from God more readily than at times of peace. Certainly, we saw this demonstrated in the days following the terrible events of September 11. It should be noted, however, that the scriptures do not say our unity is needed only at certain times. It is something for which we should always strive.

The body of Christ is comprised of a diverse collection of beings. Born-again believers come from different backgrounds, different cultures, and different ethnic groups. Our differences, being physical or otherwise manifested in tangible ways, are immediately seen. Our single commonality is spiritual and, as such, invisible. For this reason, we must make the willful determination to remember who we are in Christ, overlooking that which makes us different and embracing that which makes us one.

"Be completely humble and gentle; be patient, bearing with one another in love. Make every effort to keep the unity of the Spirit through the bond of peace." Ephesians 4:2-3 (NIV)

Questions to consider while watching the film:

1. What biblical examples illustrate the benefits of being like-minded?

2. Why, if God exhorts us to be like-minded, are there so many different Christian denominations?

Kate and Leopold
on
Wants

Film: Kate and Leopold (2001)
Directed by: James Mangold
Written by: James Mangold, Steven Rogers
U.S. Distributor: Miramax Films
Starring: Meg Ryan, Hugh Jackman, Liev Shreiber
Rated: PG-13

About the film:
A nineteenth century man time travels to twenty-first century New York. His old-fashioned chivalry draws the attention of an attractive film publicist.

Movie Quote:
"It's a great thing to get what you want. It's a really good thing unless what you thought you wanted wasn't really what you wanted. Because what you really wanted you couldn't imagine or you didn't think it was possible but what if someone came along who knew exactly what you wanted without asking?"
Kate (Meg Ryan) in Kate and Leopold (2001)

Bible Quote:
"Now to Him who is able to do immeasurably more than all we ask or imagine, according to His power that is at work within us."
Ephesians 3:20 (NIV)

Commentary:

The rambling statement that Kate makes is actually quite endearing. It expresses a desire that many of us have felt before. Who among us would not want to be loved by someone who would automatically know, without our ever telling them, exactly what we needed?

Looking into our hearts, knowing what we desire and then abundantly exceeding our expectations is something God does all the time for the people who love Him. It is a good thing too because most of the time we may think we know what we want but we are absolutely clueless as to what we really need.

We may think we know what we are missing in life. We may desire things thinking that if we had them it would somehow make us complete. But when we finally get them we find that they do not even come close to bringing us lasting happiness or joy. Indeed, they may not even be good for us. But even if they are, God is not satisfied with what is good for us. He wants what is best for us.

It truly is a great thing to have a heavenly father whose love for us surpasses our own understanding. Our God knows better than we what we need to make us complete.

Questions to consider while watching the film:

1. What are the differences between Leopold and this average modern man of today? What could be learned from him?

2. Kate, when we meet her, is extremely cynical. What has made her this way? How can we protect ourselves from becoming cynical?

The King's Speech
on
Contentment

Film: The King's Speech (2010)
Directed by: Tom Hooper
Written by: David Seidler
U.S. Distributor: The Weinstein Company
Starring: Colin Firth, Geoffrey Rush
Rated: R

About the film:
Prince Albert, known familiarly as "Bertie," is the second son of King George V and suffers from a severe speech impediment. When his older brother abdicates the throne following their father's death, the responsibility of the crown falls to Bertie who recognizes that he must overcome his physical limitation in order to be effective as a ruler.

Movie Quote:
"Poor and content is rich and rich enough."
Lionel Logue (Geoffrey Rush) In The King's Speech (2010)

Bible Quote:
"But godliness with contentment is great gain. For we brought nothing into the world, and we can take nothing out of it. But if we have food and clothing, we will be content with that."
1Timothy 6:6-8 (NIV)

Commentary:

There is great wisdom in what Lionel professes. Contentment is a state of being that is often overlooked. It never seems to be esteemed quite as highly as it deserves. In fact, most people hardly bother to give contentment a second thought. In their quest for fame, glory or riches, they neither have the time nor inclination to consider whether the attainment of those goals will truly satisfy or bring them peace.

To be content; to be satisfied in life; to be at peace with one's self and one's condition is the ultimate status symbol. It matters not if one is a king or a commoner; rich or poor, contentment is available to all who recognize and embrace its value.

The first step to contentment is to identify what our needs are. If all our needs are met, then, by simple definition, there is nothing else that we need. That is a powerful place to be. Having no need is the best kind of wealth as it brings a contentment that having all the possessions of the world cannot provide.

"Not that I speak in respect of want: for I have learned, in whatsoever state I am, therewith to be content." Philippians 4:11 (KJV)

Questions to consider while watching the film:

1. Why were Lionel's unorthodox methods successful in treating Bertie's condition?

2. There are many reasons why people have difficulty finding contentment. What are some of them?

The Kite Runner
on
Lying

Film: The Kite Runner (2007)
Directed by: Marc Forster
Written by: David Benioff
U.S. Distributor: Paramount Vantage
Starring: Khalid Abdalla, Homayoun Ershadi
Rated: PG-13

About the film:

A man returns to the land of his birth, now overtaken by religious extremists, and in doing so, must face unpleasant memories and reminders of a shame he has long carried with him.

Movie Quote:

"When you tell a lie, you steal someone's right to the truth."

Baba (Homayoun Ershadi) in The Kite Runner (2007)

Bible Quote:

"How then comfort ye me in vain, seeing in your answers there remaineth falsehood?"

Job 21:34 (KJV)

Commentary:

Baba's words of wisdom contain the seeds of truth. Lying is a form of stealing twice over. Not only is the one to whom the lie is told stolen from, the one telling the lie also suffers a loss. Peace of heart, integrity, and a satisfied soul are among the items "stolen" from a liar as he must forever carry the weight of the lie's negative and lingering effect.

Sometimes a lie may appear to be the quickest and easiest course to take in a difficult situation. It is never the right course. Whatever the justification or rationalization we may give it, a lie will never solve the problems we face. It will only exasperate them.

There can be no lasting comfort in giving someone a lie rather than the truth. Lies steal whatever strength or healing that the truth, if given, promises to provide. The world is filled with false doctrines that at one time started as small and seemingly harmless lies that people accepted and then passed along as truth.

When those lies are revealed, as all lies eventually are, those who trusted in them will be disappointed, or worse, devastated. What has been stolen from them is immeasurably greater than anything that the lie may have temporarily provided them.

Questions to consider while watching the film:

1. What was stolen from Amir and Hassan as a result of the lie?

2. Scripture states, "the truth will set you free." (John 8:32) How does that apply to this film and why?

A Knight's Tale
on
Hope

Film: A Knight's Tale (2001)
Directed by: Brian Helgeland
Written by: Brian Helgeland
U.S. Distributor: Columbia Pictures
Starring: Heath Ledger, Paul Bettany, Mark Addy
Rated: PG-13

About the film:

A young commoner takes the guise of a noble knight so that he might participate in jousting competitions. Along the way, he not only wins trophies but also the heart of a lovely lady-in-waiting. When his disguise is uncovered, and he is exposed as an imposter, he stands to lose everything he had previously gained.

Movie Quote:

"Hope guides me; that is what gets me through the day and night."
William Thatcher (Heath Ledger) in A Knight's Tale (2001)

Bible Quote:

"We have this hope as an anchor for the soul, firm and secure. It enters the inner sanctuary behind the curtain."
Hebrews 6:19 (NIV)

Commentary:

William Thatcher was a man born without means or social standing. He was taken from his home and given to a knight to serve as a squire. But despite his humble origins, he was not born without hope. His desire was to be lifted from his station so he might be viewed as a man instead of as a piece of property.

The quoted scripture compares hope to an anchor. It is a valid metaphor that paints a vivid picture. A ship without an anchor is a vessel that would not be able to hold its course when the storms hit. It would instead be left to the mercy of the prevailing winds. Likewise, a man with no hope will continually be subject to the winds of doubt and fear that blow through this world.

Hope is the belief in a future reality that has been promised. The strength of such hope is dependent upon two factors: the believing of the person to whom the promise is made and the faithfulness of the one who has promised. When those two factors are strong, our hope can indeed be strong enough to carry us through our days and nights.

Our hope, as Christians, is based upon the promises of God. There is no question of His faithfulness. May our believing be strong enough to keep our souls anchored in the harbor of His love.

Questions to consider while watching the film:

1. How did William's attitude and mindset help deliver him and lead him to the position he desired?

2. Is there any time that we could be placed in a hopeless situation? Why or why not?

Knowing
on
Prophecy

Film: Knowing (2009)

Directed by: Alex Proyas

Written by: Ryne Douglas Pearson, Juliet Snowden, Stiles White

U.S. Distributor: Summit Entertainment

Starring: Nicolas Cage, Rose Byrne

Rated: PG-13

About the film:

When a school opens a time capsule buried by students fifty years earlier, a document is uncovered that appears to accurately predict disasters and tragedies that have occurred in the years since. Unfortunately, there are a few listed in the document that have yet to come.

Movie Quote:

"I thought there was some purpose to all this. Why did I get this prediction if there's nothing I can do about it?"

John Koestler (Nicolas Cage) in Knowing (2009)

Bible Quote:

"But the manifestation of the Spirit is given to every man to profit withal."

1 Corinthians 12:7 (KJV)

Commentary:

We can understand why Koestler is feeling frustrated. To have the knowledge of future events but having neither the wisdom nor the power to act upon that knowledge would be more of a curse than a blessing.

Prophecy is one of the nine manifestations of the gift of holy spirit. As the cited scripture clearly states, all manifestations were designed by God for a profit. The specific profit or purpose to prophecy is explained in 1 Corinthians 14:3 which declares, "But the one who prophesies speaks to people for their strengthening, encouraging and comfort."

A prophecy born of God and spoken forth by a believer will always strengthen, comfort and encourage those for whom the prophecy is intended. While it is not true that a prophecy will always directly refer to future events, it will always contain messages that God wants us to hear, remember, and believe.

The prophecies of God remind us of His care, concern and interest in our lives. They inspire us to live in ways that would be pleasing to Him. They do not frustrate; they bless. They do not condemn; they comfort. They do not render us powerless; they empower us by informing or reminding us of God's promises and love for our lives.

Questions to consider while watching the film:

1. Who are the whisperers and are there any biblical similarities to their role?

2. The final twenty minutes of the film have clear references to biblical prophetic events. What are they and how well do they match the movie's depiction?

Ladyhawke
on
Human Weakness

Film: Ladyhawke (1985)
Directed by: Richard Donner
Written by: Edward Khmara, Michael Thomas, Tom Mankiewicz, David Peoples
US Distribution: Warner Brothers
Starring: Matthew Broderick, Rutger Hauer
Rated: PG-13

About the film:
A young thief is befriended by a captain and his lady love who have been cursed by a jealous bishop. Due to this curse, she becomes a hawk at daybreak and, conversely, he becomes a wolf at nightfall. The thief, Phillipe, joins them as they travel to confront the bishop and exact their revenge.

Movie Quote:
"I know I promised Lord... never again. But I also know that YOU know what a weak-willed person I am."
Phillipe (Matthew Broderick) in Ladyhawke (1985)

Bible Quote:
"As a father has compassion on his children, so the LORD has compassion on those who fear Him; for He knows how we are formed, he remembers that we are dust."
Psalms 103:13-14 (NIV)

Commentary:

Phillipe's relationship with God is both amusing and touching. He speaks to Him as he would speak to a close friend. King David, who, by revelation, wrote Psalms 103, is remembered as having the same relationship. So personal was David's relationship with his heavenly Father that he is described as being "a man after God's own heart."

God hears us when we pray and when we call out to Him in despair. He also holds us accountable for our words. After all, God would never break a promise that He has made to us. Why should He not ask that we do the same?

Of course, He knows that we will occasionally fall short in our believing and in our actions. Instead of condemning ourselves when we do, the proper course of action would be to thank God for His forgiveness and correct our behavior so that we might return to a harmonious connection with Him

Through our continual efforts to be our best for God, we will reduce the amount of time we find ourselves out of fellowship. By thinking before we speak, meaning what we say, and backing up what we say with believing action, we can grow to be the type of men and women in whom God takes great pleasure.

Questions to consider while watching the film:

1. Phillipe had an unusual personal relationship with God. What biblical personages had similar relationships?

2. Phillipe's quote was delivered while he was in the act of doing something he promised God he would not do. Does his reliance on God's understanding and forgiveness excuse his behavior? Why or why not?

Lean on Me
on
Discipline

Film: Lean On Me (1989)
Directed by: John G. Avildsen
Written by: Michael Schiffer
U.S. Distributor: Warner Brothers
Starring: Morgan Freeman, Robert Guillaume
Rated: PG-13

About the film:

Joe Clark is selected to be the principal of a run-down, inner city high school. Through sheer determination and a no-nonsense approach to education, he manages to turn the school around. In the process, he makes plenty of political enemies.

Movie Quote:

"Discipline is not the enemy of enthusiasm."

Joe Clark (Morgan Freeman) in Lean on Me (1989)

Bible Quote:

"Like a city whose walls are broken down is a man who lacks self-control."

Proverbs 25:28 (NIV)

Commentary:

It is hard to respect anything if there are no rules and no standard to indicate right from wrong. Yet the minute we identify or agree upon a standard, we automatically initiate the need for discipline to help teach us how to stay within its boundaries.

God's Word is the standard of truth. As such, it contains the reproof which helps us discipline our minds to stay within the framework which He has designed. Far from being an "enemy of enthusiasm," discipline can be a tool by which enthusiasm is increased.

No one enjoys doing something poorly. If we are taught (via instruction, reproof and correction) how to do something properly, our enthusiasm for that newly acquired skill will soar to new heights. It does so only because of the discipline which first enabled us to excel.

Without discipline, especially self-discipline (which is and has always been a learned quality), we become vulnerable to any temptation that comes our way. Temptations do little more than to draw us away from the standards of truth. It is discipline which enables us to resist the temptations and strive forward to achieve our desired goals.

Questions to consider while watching the film:

1. Joe Clark adopts some pretty severe rules in order to accomplish his goals. Was he justified? Can obedience be forced by abolishing human or civil rights?

2. Why did the students who remained in the school respond to Clark's environment of learning? How is discipline conveyed from teacher to student?

Liar, Liar
on
Lying

Film: Liar, Liar (1997)
Directed by: Tom Shadyac
Written by: Paul Guay, Stephen Mazur
U.S. Distributor: Universal Pictures
Starring: Jim Carrey, Maura Tierney, Justin Cooper
Rated: PG-13

About the film:
Fletcher, a fast-talking and somewhat unscrupulous lawyer, discovers that he has lost the ability to lie when his long-neglected five-year-old son makes an unusual birthday wish. Unfortunately for Fletcher, he has just been handed an important case that he believes cannot be won unless he is allowed to bend the truth just a little.

Movie Quote:
"I wish, for just one day, Dad couldn't tell a lie."
Max Reede (Justin Cooper) in Liar, Liar (1997)

Bible Quote:
"God is not a man, that He should lie, nor a son of man, that He should change His mind. Does He speak and then not act? Does He promise and not fulfill?"
Numbers 23:19 (NIV)

Commentary:

To anyone blessed with children, Max's wish in "Liar, Liar" is especially heartbreaking. How unstable and insecure would life be if we could not trust the one into whose trust we have been given? Fathers are supposed to tell us the truth. At the heart of Max's wish is his desire to believe the person who is supposed to love him the most. It is a desire we all share.

We are blessed with the knowledge that our spiritual Father is, in fact, incapable of lying. It is simply not in His divine nature. He is all truth, all light and all love. And He cannot lie. (Titus 1:2)

Because we can trust Him to tell the truth always, we can trust in His Word implicitly. Such trust brings peace to our hearts and joy to our lives. We have the key to life and happiness. As God assures us, truth really shall make us free. (John 8:32)

Because He committed His Word to a written form which we can read, study, and apply, He has given us a foundation of unshakable truth upon which we might build our lives. It is a foundation upon which we may trust without doubt or hesitation. It shall never fail nor disappoint us. The truth shall stand for all time. And we shall prevail as we believe and act upon it.

Questions to consider while watching the film:

1. Why do people lie? What arguments can be made to counter their rationalizations?

2. One of Fletcher's problems lies in his prioritizing his life. What is the proper priority we should take between the following: a) our jobs; b) our family; c) our relationship with God?

The Man in the Iron Mask
on
Leaders

Film: The Man in the Iron Mask (1998)
Directed by: Randall Wallace
Written by: Randall Wallace
U.S. Distributor: United Artists
Starring: Leonardo DiCaprio, John Malkovich
Rated: PG-13

About the film:
The evil Louis XIV rules France with an iron fist and a cold heart. The famous Three Musketeers have long since retired, disillusioned by the king they once served so honorably. But when they learn that the king has imprisoned his twin, they forge a daring plan to rescue all of France from the ruling tyrant.

Movie Quote:
"But we all had a common dream. That one day we would serve a king worthy of the throne."
Athos (John Malkovich) in The Man in the Iron Mask (1998)

Bible Quote:
"They will make war against the Lamb, but the Lamb will overcome them because he is Lord of lords and King of kings – and with him will be his called, chosen and faithful followers."
Revelation 17:14 (NIV)

Commentary:

Like Athos, we know all too well the disappointment of following a leader who fails to live up to expectations. Greed, lust, and fear are just some of the human frailties that have caused many a great man to falter and fail.

When a leader succumbs to his weaknesses, those who follow him and have trusted in him for guidance, strength and stability can be shaken to their core. They can begin to doubt the assurance and conviction they once held regarding even the most fundamental of their beliefs.

Regardless of the actions of the men with whom we choose to stand, the foundation of our faith need not be weakened. This is because we do not build our hope upon what men may say or do. Our hope and trust is built upon promises made by God who is faithful and true. He tells us that there is a king coming who is worthy of his throne. We may begin serving him today by accepting him as our Lord and adopting his ways as our own.

Questions to consider while watching the film:

1. What was the mental and emotional condition of each of the Musketeers at the beginning of the film? How did they get like that? What caused them to change?

2. Near the end of the film, as the cornered Musketeers charge into the battalion of armed soldiers, why were the soldiers unable to shoot straight? What does this teach us about facing our obstacles and adversaries?

The Matrix
on
Believing

Film: The Matrix (1999)
Directed by: Andy Wachowski, Larry Wachowski
Written by: Andy Wachowski, Larry Wachowski
U.S. Distributor: Warner Brothers
Starring: Keanu Reeves, Laurence Fishburne
Rated: R

About the film:
A computer hacker named Neo discovers that the world he thought he knew is a facade. Machines have built a complex system capable of hiding the true nature of life from the eyes of all but a few renegade men. Neo joins forces with these rebels to fight against the machines who aim to keep all of humanity under their control.

Movie Quote:
"You have to let it all go, Neo. Fear, doubt, and disbelief. Free your mind."
Morpheus (Laurence Fishburne) in The Matrix (1999)

Bible Quote:
"'If you can?' said Jesus. Everything is possible for him who believes."
Mark 9:23 (NIV)

Commentary:

In "The Matrix," Morpheus teaches Neo the importance of believing with one's whole heart. If we could learn only one thing in this world, the principle of believing would be the most important. What we choose to believe is the reality in which we live.

It is our believing that activates the power of God. As we faithfully take the truth we believe and apply it to our situations of life, we receive the results that He promises. Allowing doubt, fear, worry, or disbelief to take residence in our minds only serves to remove us from that abundant free-flowing stream of blessings that God is always willing and able to give us.

Freeing our minds from disbelief is a deliberate act of will that requires discipline, study, and a continual effort. "Blind faith" too often fails because it is weak. It has no solid foundation of truth or understanding. A strong faith born of a spiritual understanding based upon one's study of God's Word (and one's proving of His Word through application and practice) is far more rewarding. It is why God so often exhorts us to know and do His commandments.

Questions to consider while watching the film:

1. If everything is possible, why do we not see miracles every day?

2. Neo had to grow into his level of understanding and believing. We must do the same in our lives. What are the techniques that can be employed to help us get past our disbelief? What examples from the film support your answer?

The Matrix Reloaded
on
Purpose

Film: The Matrix Reloaded (2003)
Directed by: Andy Wachowski, Larry Wachowski
Written by: Andy Wachowski, Larry Wachowski
Studio: Warner Brothers
Starring: Keanu Reeves, Carrie-Anne Moss
Rated: R

About the film:
The second film of the sci-fi trilogy finds the remaining "unplugged" humans fighting for their life and freedom against the machines that have tried to enslave them within a complex computerized matrix.

Movie Quote:
"Because as we both know, without purpose, we would not exist. It is purpose that created us; purpose that connects us; purpose that pulls us. That guides us. That drives us. It is purpose that defines us. Purpose that binds us."
Smith (Hugo Weaving) in The Matrix: Reloaded (2003)

Bible Quote:
"In Him we were also chosen, having been predestined according to the plan of Him who works out everything in conformity with the purpose of His will."
Ephesians 1:11 (NIV)

Commentary:

Agent Smith may be the villain in this film but he shows a remarkable awareness of a fundamental truth. That truth, simply put, is that there is a reason for our existence; a purpose to which we were called.

It does not take faith to understand that there is an order to this world. The evidence is all around us, woven into the very fabric of creation. For order to exist there must be structure. With structure comes reason and intelligence and, of course, purpose.

God designed and created this world for a singular purpose; to give a place where you and I could live and grow. He created everything that exists. Everything that we can see, smell, hear, taste, and touch was created for the expressed purpose of supporting and enriching our lives.

His motivation, simply expressed, was love. Love is what He desires and it is all He expects from us in return. It makes perfect sense to recognize that love is our purpose or reason to live.

"Love the Lord your God with all your heart and with all your soul and with all your mind and with all your strength." Mark 12:30 (NIV)

Questions to consider while watching the film:

1. Why is having a purpose important to our lives?

2. How can we best discover what our purpose is?

Mississippi Burning
on
Hatred

Film: Mississippi Burning (1988)
Directed by: Alan Parker
Written by: Chris Gerolmo
U.S. Distributor: Orion Pictures Corporation
Starring: Gene Hackman, Willem Dafoe
Rated: R

About the film:
When three young civil rights workers disappear in
Mississippi during a voter registration drive, two FBI
agents are sent to investigate. They learn that they must
sort through the prevalent racial bigotry existing within
the community before they can hope to uncover the truth
behind the disappearance.

Movie Quote:
"Hatred isn't something you're born with. It gets taught."
Mrs. Pell (Frances McDormand) in Mississippi Burning
(1988)

Bible Quote:
"But whoever hates his brother is in the darkness and
walks around in the darkness; he does not know where he
is going, because the darkness has blinded him."
1 John 2:11 (NIV)

Commentary:

Hatred comes in all forms, whether it is the racial prejudice of which Mrs. Pell is speaking or an animosity towards someone for more personal reasons. What all hatred has in common is the fact that it stands in direct opposition and contrast to the lessons of Christ.

That comes as no surprise. This world tries to "teach" us many things that we would be better off not learning. God does not give lessons in how to hate. The promotion of such a negative and unprofitable waste of energy can only come from a teacher who does not want us to succeed.

We need not take our lessons from this world. We certainly are not to conform to the world's way of thinking or behaving. We are blessed to have another teacher from whom to learn. We have an instructor whose lessons of love, peace, joy and forgiveness are designed to fill our hearts and guide our steps.

The darkness which blinds people and keeps them from learning the ways that will lead to a better, more productive and happier life is easy to overcome. It must flee the moment someone turns on a light. In God's classroom, the lights are never dimmed.

Questions to consider while watching the film:

1. Where does hate come from? What is its connection to fear?

2. What is the proper response to hatred that may be directed towards us?

Moonstruck
on
Women

Film: Moonstruck (1987)
Directed by: Norman Jewison
Written by: John Patrick Shanley
U.S. Distributor: MGM
Starring: Cher, Nicolas Cage, Olympia Dukakis
Rated: PG

About the film:
A widowed Brooklyn bookkeeper decides that it is time she gets married again but she becomes confused over which guy to join in wedlock: the nice guy whom she does not love; or his passionately intense brother whom she barely knows.

Movie Quote:
"Now maybe, just maybe, a man isn't complete as a man without a woman."
Johnny (Danny Aiello) in Moonstruck (1987)

Bible Quote:
"But the woman is the glory of man. For man did not come from woman, but woman from man."
1 Corinthians 11:7b-8 (NIV)

Commentary:

There is no maybe about it. The Bible is clear in stating that the whole reason for woman's existence was to complete the man. Had woman not been created, God's work would have been imperfect and that is not only unthinkable, it would be impossible.

God made Eve to be a help designed specifically for the man. Eve was not created first nor was God's work completed after making Adam. After each one of God's wondrous works, which are recorded in the first chapter of Genesis, the scriptures state that "it was good." After making Adam, God, for the first time, declared that something He created was not good. "It is not good that the man should be alone." (Genesis 2:18)

This unique relationship between a man and a woman is further explored by God's description of the ultimate union between them. God describes marriage as a mystery in Ephesians 5, referring to how two people can become "one flesh." For those who have never experienced it, it can be difficult to fully understand. For those who have, it can be difficult to imagine living life any other way.

Questions to consider while watching the film:

1. What are the qualifications one should seek in a marriage partner?

2. What do the infidelities of the characters say about love and about the weaknesses of the human spirit? How can we guard ourselves against sexual temptation?

Mr. Deeds
on
Fools

Film: Mr. Deeds (2002)
Directed by: Steven Brill
Written by: Tim Herlihy
U.S. Distributor: Columbia Pictures
Starring: Adam Sandler, Winona Ryder
Rated: PG-13

About the film:
Longfellow Deeds is a simple man from a small New England town who not only inherits a fortune but also controlling interest in a huge multi-media conglomerate. He travels to the big city where his small town ways make him vulnerable to the ruthless, unethical and self-serving people he encounters there.

Movie Quote:
"It's hard to soar with the eagles when you're surrounded by turkeys."
Mr. Deeds (Adam Sandler) in Mr. Deeds (2002)

Bible Quote:
"He who walks with the wise grows wise, but a companion of fools suffers harm."
1 Corinthians 15:33 (NIV)

Commentary:

Deeds may be a simple man but simple men often have a way of seeing things more clearly than so-called "complex thinkers." Deed's quoted comment is not only amusing but ultimately rings true. Like it or not, we are affected by those with whom we choose to associate. Hanging around with a bunch of flightless "turkeys" can easily keep us from realizing our true potential as eagles.

We are, from an early age, exhorted to "choose our friends wisely." As we mature, we come to realize the wisdom of that advice. There have been many people with a promising future who never reached the fullness of their potential because they followed the advice or direction of the wrong people. Some of the worst decisions we make in life are a direct result of the peer pressure we experience from those we unwisely choose as our friends or companions.

Fortunately, the converse is also true. We can choose to fellowship with those who demonstrate positive or admirable traits. When we do, this beneficial association tends to rub off on us as well. We can learn from and can be guided by their example; we can be encouraged by their successes; and we can be inspired by their character. We can soar in this life with a little help from our friends.

Questions to consider while watching the film:

1. Who in the Bible erred as a result of the company he or she kept?

2. What are the benefits of fellowshipping with like-minded believers? How is this reflected in the film?

The Natural
on
Natural Abilities

Film: The Natural (1984)

Directed by: Barry Levinson

Written by: Roger Towne, Phil Dusenberry

U.S. Distributor: TriStar Pictures

Starring: Robert Redford, Glenn Close

Rated: PG

About the film:

Roy Hobbs was a promising new baseball talent whose fast-track career was derailed by a chance encounter. Now, at the age when most men retire from the sport, Roy is trying to start again.

Movie Quote:

"You've got a gift, Roy, but it's not enough. You've got to develop yourself. Rely too much on your own gift and you'll fail."

Ed Hobbs (Alan Fudge) in The Natural (1984)

Bible Quote:

"Trust in the LORD with all your heart and lean not on your own understanding."

Proverbs 3:5 (NIV)

Commentary:

Hobbs' father is teaching his son some valuable truths that can be applied far beyond the game of baseball. Having a natural aptitude for something is a great asset but it is only a beginning. It is available to reach beyond one's self and achieve even greater results.

Our natural abilities, no matter how impressive, are inherently limited. As soon as we recognize that there is a source of strength, wisdom and power outside of us and into which we can tap, we are able to add to our limited abilities an unlimited supply of power and knowledge. We then enter into a brand new realm of limitless potential.

God's vision for us will always be greater than the vision we have for ourselves. We often forget the many resources that we have at our disposal. We have spiritual resources that, if utilized, could enable us to achieve greater things. God never forgets them. And He continually tries to remind us that, no matter how good we may be at something, when we involve Him in our lives, we are infinitely better.

Questions to consider while watching the film:

1. Consider the role women play in this film. Discuss both the positive and negative attributes they demonstrate and compare them to scriptural examples.

2. Why did the Knights start playing better as a team once Roy Hobbs started to play with them? What spiritual truths does this bring to mind?

Nixon
on
Resentment

Film: Nixon (1995)
Directed by: Oliver Stone
Written by: Stephen J. Rivels, Christopher Wilkinson, Oliver Stone
U.S. Distributor: Buena Vista Pictures
Starring: Anthony Hopkins, Joan Allen
Rated: R

About the film:
Beginning with the Watergate burglary, this film traces the presidency of Richard Milhous Nixon, the only U.S. President to resign from his office to avoid impeachment proceedings.

Movie Quote:
"Always remember: others may hate you. But those who hate you don't win unless you hate them. And then you destroy yourself."
Richard M. Nixon (Anthony Hopkins) in Nixon (1995)

Bible Quote:
"If people do not welcome you, shake the dust off your feet when you leave their town, as a testimony against them."
Luke 9:5 (NIV)

Commentary:

We do not live for God in order to win a popularity contest. If we do, we have some unpleasant surprises in store for us. Jesus was very direct in his instruction to his disciples. There are those in this world who would rather we never said a single word or performed a single action that would further the movement of God's Word.

But we do not live to please those of this world. We do what we do to please God. It is His good pleasure that directs us to hold forth His truth to all men.

Not everyone will welcome the good news we have to share. But to respond to hatred or resentment with the same is not the course of action God would have us take. He has given us instruction that we can follow whenever we come across someone who is less than blessed with our presence.

The phrase "shaking the dust from your feet" in Luke 9:5 is an oriental figure of speech that means to hold no resentment or bitterness. We are to continually operate from a mindset of love and service. All we can do is to hold forth the truth. If someone does not want to hear it, we can simply move on to someone who does.

Questions to consider while watching the film:

1. What character traits of Richard Nixon led to his downfall?

2. The film opens by quoting from Matthew 16:26. How could this verse have helped Nixon? What elements of our lives or actions might we consider changing in light of that scripture?

The Notebook
on
Love

Film: The Notebook (2004)
Directed by: Nick Cassavetes
Written by: Jeremy Levin
U.S. Distributor: New Line Cinema
Starring: Ryan Gosling, Rachel McAdams
Rated: PG-13

About the film:
Two love stories, taking place generations apart, are being told simultaneously. In one, a young man falls in love with a young girl who is from a higher social class but he still pursues her diligently. In the other, an older man visits a nursing center where he reads a book to an invalid. The stories eventually intertwine and speak volumes about the capacity of love, forgiveness, and hope.

Movie Quote:
"The best love is the kind that awakens the soul and makes us reach for more."
Noah Calhoun (Ryan Gosling) in The Notebook (2004)

Bible Quote:
"Beloved, if God so loved us, we ought also to love one another."
1 John 4:11 (KJV)

Commentary:

Love, as it has been said, makes the world go round. It is at or should be at the very core of our being. Without love, life has little meaning and less importance. But there are, as Noah implies, different kinds of love.

Looking at the scriptures, we can see that this is true. Love is a central theme throughout the Bible but to appreciate it fully, we must look beyond the English all-inclusive word for love to gain a better understanding. We know of brotherly love, affectionate love, physical love, and maternal or paternal love. But all these different kinds of love pale in comparison to the greatest love of all – agape love.

Agape, one of the Greek words translated as love in the English Bible, refers to the kind of love our heavenly Father extends to us. Unselfish, all-giving, all-encompassing, it is a love that overwhelms the senses and leaves us with a burning desire to pass it along. It is unquenchable, fathomless, and undeniable. With agape love at the heart of our life's endeavors, we cannot fail. God's love awakens our soul and leaves us longing for more.

Questions to consider while watching the film:

1. How is love illustrated in the film? Who is closest to achieving the "agape" love that is so desirable?

2. What other godly qualities are demonstrated by the characters in the film? At what times are the characters at their best? When are they at their worst? What can we learn from this?

O Brother, Where Art Thou?
on
Logic

Film: O Brother, Where Art Thou? (2000)
Directed by: Joel Coen
Written by: Ethan Coen, Joel Coen
U.S. Distributor: Buena Vista Pictures
Starring: George Clooney, John Turturro
Rated: PG-13

About the film:
Loosely based upon Homer's "Odyssey" and set in the 1920s, three convicts escape from a work crew and set off in pursuit of the loot one of them has stashed away. Oddly enough, during their journey, they become singing sensations and meet up with "Babyface" Nelson.

Movie Quote:
"It's a fool who looks for logic in the chambers of the human heart."
McGill (George Clooney) in O Brother, Where Art Thou? (2000)

Bible Quote:
"He that trusteth in his own heart is a fool: but whoso walketh wisely, he shall be delivered."
Proverbs 28:26 (NIV)

Commentary:

Logic, as defined by Webster's Dictionary, is a system of reasoning; the process by which rational thought is achieved. To reason, one must draw from knowledge originating outside of one's own self.

We believe in God, but not in response to an emotional reaction or feeling. Such "faith," when tested, would never be able to stand because it lacks a truly solid foundation. We know God to exist simply because we logically conclude it to be true. That conclusion is based not upon what we feel in our hearts but rather upon our study and application of the Word which God recorded and made available to us.

The Word of God (itself called "logos" in the Greek language) contains the standard of truth from which logical thought may be built. As we learn and understand more of His Word, our believing is strengthened, our thoughts become sound, and our logic is unmatched. God has provided us with a solid foundation upon which we may build our entire lives. When we continue to build upon that foundation, He promises that our lives will be more than abundant.

Questions to consider while watching the film:

1. "O Brother Where Art Thou?" is something of a redemptive tale. In what ways is this manifested in the story?

2. Often, the scriptures use the word "fool" to describe someone who turns from God or does not believe and trust in Him. How does that compare to McGill's description of a fool?

Once Upon a Time…
When We Were Colored
on
Study

Film: Once Upon a Time…When We Were Colored (1995)
Directed by: Tim Reid
Written by: Paul W Cooper
U.S. Distributor: Republic Pictures
Starring: Al Freeman Jr., Phylicia Rashad, Paula Kelly
Rated: PG

About the film:

A tightly knit black community must make a decision regarding racial discrimination when one of their own is being persecuted by a white businessman who is in competition with him.

Movie Quote:

"Books are like eggs. You got to crack 'em open to get anything out of them."
Miss Maybry (Polly Bergen) in Once Upon a Time… When We Were Colored (1995)

Bible Quote:

"In reading this, then, you will be able to understand my insight into the mystery of Christ."
Ephesians 3:4 (NIV)

Commentary:

Miss Maybry gives a simple yet powerful illustration. Most of the time, in order to get what we want, it requires an action on our part. Sitting and waiting for something to come to us is a sure way to be disappointed in this life.

God has recorded that He has given us all things pertaining to life and godliness. And He has. They are contained within the pages of the Bible. Because of this, the Bible is a source of incredible power but if we never read it or study what it contains, it remains a lifeless object.

Similarly, we can sit in our cars all day long, but if we never get behind the wheel, turn the key, put the car into gear and press on the accelerator, we will not be going anyplace. It takes action on our part for the power of the car to become evident.

The same principle holds true with the Word of God. Only when we read and study the Word; when we believe and claim its promises; and when we act according to our believing, will the power of God become evident. Do not let the Bible be just another dust-covered book on a long-forgotten shelf. Crack open the pages and discover the power within.

Questions to consider while watching the film:

1. God often communicates His truth to us by using analogies or comparative illustrations to help us remember them. What are some that come to mind?

2. A major theme in the film is the effects of racial prejudice. Upon what is prejudice based and what is the best way to diffuse it?

Patch Adams
on
Problem Solving

Film: Patch Adams (1998)
Directed by: Tom Shadyac
Written by: Steve Oedekerk
U.S. Distributor: Universal Pictures
Starring: Robin Williams, Monica Potter
Rated: PG-13

About the film:
A medical student adopts a rather unorthodox method of treating the sick. In order to practice these methods, he decides to open his own clinic in which he tries to break down the invisible, emotional barrier between patient and doctor.

Movie Quote:
"You're focusing on the problem. If you focus on the problem, you can't see the solution. Never focus on the problem."
Arthur Mendelson (Harold Gould) in Patch Adams (1998)

Bible Quote:
"Without weakening in his faith, he faced the fact that his body was as good as dead – since he was about a hundred years old – and that Sarah's womb was also dead. Yet he did not waver through unbelief regarding the promise of God, but was strengthened in his faith and gave glory to God."
Romans 4:19-20 (NIV)

MICHAEL ELLIOTT

Commentary:

Sometimes profound statements will be made by secondary or inconsequential characters. Arthur Mendelson had only a few moments of screen time but his words speak volumes.

A successful runner will not, in the middle of his race, look down at his feet and wonder why they are not moving faster. He instead keeps his eyes focused ahead, towards the finish line, where victory awaits.

God promised Abraham that he would be the "father of many nations." As he neared the age of one hundred, he was still childless. His wife, Sarah, was ninety. It would have been easy for them to believe the physical conditions of their aging bodies. They chose instead to keep their minds focused on God's promise. They received the victory because God kept His promise despite the "physical impossibilities."

Focusing on the reasons why something cannot be done is often the primary reason why things do not get done. Victory and deliverance are promised to us. Let us turn our eyes away from that which holds us back and focus instead on that which will draw us forward.

Questions to consider while watching the film:

1. Success or victory is largely dependent upon attitude. How is this truth reflected in the film?

2. Scripture says that a cheerful heart is good medicine. Does the film support that truth? How?

126

The Preacher's Wife
on
Believing

Film: The Preacher's Wife (1996)

Directed by: Penny Marshall

Written by: Nat Mauldin, Allan Scott

Studio: Buena Vista Pictures

Starring: Denzel Washington, Whitney Houston

Rated: PG

About the film:

A hardworking reverend is allowing his marriage to falter because of the constant pressures of his work and the financial difficulties of his church. He prays to God for help but the angel who arrives as his answer to prayer seems to be making matters worse.

Movie Quote:

"Just because you can't see the air doesn't keep you from breathing. And just because you can't see God doesn't keep you from believing."

Jeremiah Biggs (Justin Pierre Edmund) in The Preacher's Wife (1996)

Bible Quote:

"We live by faith, not by sight."

2 Corinthians 5:7 (NIV)

Commentary:

"The Preacher's Wife" presents us with a story which, for some, can be hard to believe. The scriptures do speak of angels and describe angelic encounters that men have had. That does not mean that it is easy to embrace the concept of an angel appearing before us.

There is no question that it is easier to believe what is right before our faces than it is to believe something that is invisible. If we think about it however, there are many things in this world that we know exist even though we have never been able to see them.

The quote from "The Preacher's Wife" identifies one. Air cannot be seen yet we have no doubt that when we inhale, we replenish our lungs with that substance required of all human life. Likewise, when we get out of bed each morning, we are confident that our feet will remain on the floor because of an invisible reality called gravity.

We believe in these things that we cannot see because we can see the effects caused by their existence. If we are spiritually attuned, we will also see the effects of the invisible God who is every bit as real and vital as the air and gravity which He created.

Questions to consider while watching the film:

1. How can we believe in that which we cannot see? How can we build our faith?

2. The angel does not seem to immediately satisfy the prayers of Rev. Biggs. Why not? What does this teach us about how God answers prayers?

Ratatouille
on
Decisions

Film: Ratatouille (2007)

Directed by: Brad Bird, Jan Pinkava

Written by: Brad Bird, Jan Pinkava, Jim Capobianco

U.S. Distributor: Buena Vista Pictures

Starring: Patton Oswalt, Lou Romano, Brad Garrett

Rated: G

About the film:

A young rodent has a passion for cooking and finds himself with the unique opportunity to showcase his culinary skills at a famous French restaurant. But, though his food is heavenly, will anyone be willing to eat a meal prepared by a sewer rat?

Movie Quote:

"Change is nature, the part that we can influence, and it starts when we decide."

Remy (Patton Oswalt) in Ratatouille (2007)

Bible Quote:

"I know thy works, that thou art neither cold nor hot: I would thou wert cold or hot."

Revelation 3:15 (KJV)

Commentary:

The key to Remy's comment is found in the latter part of his quote, "…it starts when we decide." Because God granted us the incredible power of free will, our decisions become the launching pad for great things to take place in our lives.

The four Ds of a disciplined life are (in order of their occurrence): Decision, Desire, Details, and Deliverance. We decide to believe or to take an action. Based on that decision, we begin to desire to see the results of the decision. We then must faithfully work through the details of the action(s) required by our initial decision. And, in time, we will receive the results or the deliverance that is promised by our God. These godly results will only be achieved after we first make a decision.

Often, we may try to skip the decision-making step to let desire rule our lives. That is always a grievous mistake. God gave us free will and a sound mind to exercise it. When we do according to His standards, the results will please God and greatly exceed our own expectations. When we do not, we open ourselves up to two more Ds - deception and disappointment.

Questions to consider while watching the film:

1. What decisions had to be made by the characters in this film for the story to have the happy ending it did?

2. The film's catch phrase, "Anyone Can Cook," can be modified and applied to a Christian viewpoint. What scriptures indicate God's willingness to accept anyone into His family?

The Razor's Edge
on
Jesus Christ

Film: The Razor's Edge (1984)
Directed by: John Byrum
Written by: John Byrum, Bill Murray
U.S. Distributor: Columbia Pictures
Starring: Bill Murray, Theresa Russell
Rated: PG-13

About the film:
A World War I veteran is emotionally changed by his battlefield experiences. He returns home to his fiancée but cannot find peace of heart. He leaves her to seek for the meaning of life, traveling from Paris to Tibet. The next time he and his fiancée meet, their relationship has been irrevocably changed.

Movie Quote:
"The pathway to salvation is as narrow and as difficult to walk as a razor's edge."
A Tibetan monk in The Razor's Edge (1984)

Bible Quote:
"But small is the gate and narrow the road that leads to life, and only a few find it."
 Matthew 7:14 (NIV)

Commentary:

The wise Tibetan monk who spoke that line in "The Razor's Edge" did not understand or believe in the all-knowing, all-forgiving heart of God. Yes, the way to salvation is "narrow" but it is not as impossible to traverse as a razor's edge. The reason it is called "narrow" is because while there is only one "way" to salvation, there are numerous "ways" that lead away from it.

The one way to life everlasting can be found in the understanding of and believing in Jesus Christ. All other theories, beliefs, postulations, and fantasies will lead people to nothing more than dead ends. If the Bible is true, as it is when it is properly read and "rightly divided," Jesus Christ is the key to all spiritual understanding.

When we confess Jesus as Lord in our life and believe that God raised him from the dead, we will have found and opened that small gate that leads to eternal life. Anything else leads to oblivion. Jesus himself said that "I am the way, the truth, and the life. No man comes unto the Father but by me." (John 14:6) We can trust those words and believe them for they are true.

Questions to consider while watching the film:

1. The central character desires to know the meaning of life. How does God answer this question in His Word?

2. Life experiences will cause us to grow and change. How can we best manage our relationships with our spouses so we do not grow apart?

Rock Star
on
Diligence

Film: Rock Star (2001)

Directed by: Stephen Herek

Written by: John Stockwell

U.S. Distributor: Warner Brothers

Starring: Mark Wahlberg, Jennifer Aniston

Rated: R

About the film:

When the lead singer of a famous rock band is voted out of his group, an average guy who sings in a garage cover band is given his shot at mega-stardom. He learns that having fame is not the same as handling it.

Movie Quote:

"That's right, I'm standing here, living proof that if you work hard enough, and you want it bad enough... dreams do come true. So, follow your dreams."

Chris (Mark Wahlberg) in Rock Star (2001)

Bible Quote:

"The sluggard craves and gets nothing, but the desires of the diligent are fully satisfied."

Proverbs 13:4 (NIV)

Commentary:

Just because we might want something does not necessarily mean we will get it. This world is filled with people who are continually disappointed in their expectations. We do not have to count ourselves as being among them.

Using this film as an illustration of this truth, we see that Chris respected the music produced by the rock group, Steel Dragon. He respected them so much that he worked hard to emulate their sound. Because of his hard work and tireless efforts, when the opportunity came knocking, he was ready to answer.

God's promises will always work for those who are not only faithful to believe them but also diligent to act upon their believing. Working heartily, as unto the Lord, is a key element to having a prosperous life.

As we set our hearts upon desired goals, we are to relentlessly work towards those goals, having no doubt that our victory is assured. Our patience, faithfulness and diligence will ultimately be rewarded as we receive and enjoy the fruits of our labor. God is able to not only meet our desires, but abundantly exceed them.

Questions to consider while watching the film:

1. What was it about Chris that drew the band's attention to him? Why was he given the lead singer's spot?

2. After being hired by the group, where did Chris go wrong? What did he forget? What lessons can be learned from his experiences?

134

Rocky IV
on
Change

Film: Rocky IV (1985)
Directed by: Sylvester Stallone
Written by: Sylvester Stallone
U.S. Distributor: MGM/UA Entertainment
Starring: Sylvester Stallone, Talia Shire, Burt Young
Rated: PG

About the film:
After his friend, Apollo Creed, is killed in a bout with the chemically enhanced Soviet fighter Ivan Drago, Rocky agrees to fight the Russian on his home turf. During the grueling match, Rocky learns something about himself and the nature of people.

Movie Quote:
"I guess what I'm trying to say is, if I can change, and you can change, everybody can change."
Rocky Balboa (Sylvester Stallone) in Rocky IV (1985)

Bible Quote:
"Repent then, and turn to God, so that your sins may be wiped out, that times of refreshing may come from the Lord."
Acts 3:19 (NIV)

Commentary:

Rocky expresses one of the fundamental blessings which God makes available to man. We have the right to change and grow, not only as individuals but as spiritual beings.

Spiritually, we all start from the same place. We are born as individuals "having no hope, and without God in the world." (Ephesians 2:12) How then do we gain a relationship with God and access to all His promises? Very simply, we must change. And because God is a loving Creator, He has given each and every man, woman and child the free will ability to do so.

The instant we confess Jesus as Lord and believe in our hearts that God has raised him from the dead (Romans 10:9-10), we are changed. We move from being a "natural man" with body and soul, to a threefold being: body, soul and spirit. God restores us to complete wholeness by creating within us the "earnest (token) of our inheritance" (Ephesians 1:14) which is spirit.

Since God is spirit (John 4:24), our change is essential if we are to join in full fellowship with Him, His son Jesus Christ, and all who call upon the name of the Lord. Change can be a good thing and when we are speaking of a spiritual change it will be the best decision we could ever make.

Questions to consider while watching the film:

1. Note the differences between the way Ivan Drago trains and the way Rocky trains. Which is more rewarding and why?

2. What was it that got the crowd to change its opinion of Rocky? What can we learn from that?

Roxanne

on

Knowledge

Film: Roxanne (1987)
Directed by: Fred Schepisi
Written by: Steve Martin
U.S. Distributor: Columbia Pictures
Starring: Steve Martin, Daryl Hannah
Rated: PG

About the film:

"Roxanne" is a modern version of Edmond Rostand's play, "Cyrano de Bergerac." In it, fire chief C.D. Bales is blessed with a sharp mind, a quick wit, and an extraordinarily large nose. His affections are fixed on the beautiful Roxanne. She only has eyes for the dimwitted but handsome Chris.

Movie Quote:

"Sometimes, the answer is so obvious, that it's as plain as the nose on your face."
Dixie (Shelly Duvall) in Roxanne (1987)

Bible Quote:

"For this commandment which I command thee this day, it is not hidden from thee, neither is it far off."
 Deuteronomy 30:11 (KJV)

MICHAEL ELLIOTT

Commentary:

C.D. Bales' biggest problem is that he cannot see beyond the problem he is convinced he has. If he could, he would see the solution that is so obvious to Dixie and to the rest of us.

But we should not think badly of C.D. In many ways, we share the same affliction. We have all had questions that we have wanted answered. We have questions about life, death, love, and God that we spend our lifetimes thinking about without realizing that the answers were always available to us, and just as plain as the nose on our face.

The Bible says that God has given us all things pertaining to life and godliness. The answers we seek, He has provided. God originally set them in the stars for all to see. He gave them directly to Adam and commanded that they be passed down from father to son throughout the generations. He caused them to be recorded in a written form. And finally, He gave them to us by sending us His only begotten son to teach us.

If our questions are still going unanswered, it is not God's doing. He has not hidden the answers from us. We simply need to look at what He has given us. Instead of stumbling in the dark, we need only turn to the light that has always been there.

Questions to consider while watching the film:

1. Why do some men choose to stay in spiritual darkness when light is available?

2. How does fear manifest itself in the actions of the characters? What is the result of that fear?

Shadowlands
on
Prayer

Film: Shadowlands (1993)
Directed by: Richard Attenborough
Written by: William Nicholson
U.S. Distributor: Savoy Pictures
Starring: Anthony Hopkins, Debra Winger
Rated: PG

About the film:
C.S. Lewis, a professor at Oxford University and Christian author of children's books, begins a romance with a free-spirited American fan named Joy. Their romance comes to a bittersweet end when Joy is diagnosed with a terminal illness.

Movie Quote:
"I pray because I can't help myself. I pray because I'm helpless. I pray because the need flows out of me all the time, waking and sleeping. It doesn't change God, it changes me."
C.S. Lewis (Anthony Hopkins) in Shadowlands (1993)

Bible Quote:
"Therefore confess your sins to each other and pray for each other so that you may be healed. The prayer of a righteous man is powerful and effective."
James 5:16 (NIV)

Commentary:

C.S. Lewis offers a beautiful expression of how he views prayer. By saying that "it doesn't change God, it changes me," he speaks a profound truth that, once recognized, may forever change the manner in which we pray.

What is the value of prayer? Why should we ask God to do things for us that we cannot do for ourselves? If God loves us and He knows the desires of our hearts, why does He not act on our behalf regardless of what we do or say?

The answer should be obvious. Among the laws of the universe which He has designed, God has given us free will. Certainly He wants us to have what He knows is best for us but He cannot contradict His own immutable laws. He has given us free will which means that He must wait until we welcome Him into our lives.

Praying to God softens our hearts and attitude. God is constant. He is always good and He is always giving. We are the variable ones in this equation. His desire is always to bless us. But He cannot give until we bridge the gulf between us and demonstrate our willingness to receive.

Questions to consider while watching the film:

1. One key to prayer can be found in Mark 11:24. Consider C.S. Lewis's quote from the context of this verse.

2. Why do some prayers seem to go unnoticed? What is the key to maintaining our faith in the face of tragedies or disappointments?

Shall We Dance?
on
Confidence

Film: Shall We Dance? (1996)
Directed by: Masayuki Suo
Written by: Masayuki Suo
U.S. Distributor: Miramax Films
Starring: Koji Yakusho, Tamiyo Kusakari
Rated: PG

About the film:

A Japanese businessman, suffering from a severe case of ennui, rediscovers the joy and excitement in life when he begins secretly taking ballroom dance lessons. It is a practice that is not immediately understood or appreciated in the button-down world in which he lives.

Movie Quote:

"A weak first step transmits nothing."
Mia Kishikawa (Tamiyo Kusakari) in Shall We Dance? (1996)

Bible Quote:

"He makes my feet like the feet of a deer; he causes me to stand on the heights."
 2 Samuel 22:34 (NIV)

Commentary:

We see, as we watch Shohei learn the fundamentals of ballroom dance, the importance of firm and confident actions. A dance between two people is an artful form of communication and, as in any type of communication, it is important to make sure the proper message is being received.

Properly leading a dance partner requires confidence and deliberate, well-defined actions. Hesitant or tentative movements will not communicate to a partner and will spoil the dance before it starts. Our Christian walk is no different.

When we believe fully, our movements are sure and our expectation of success is high. As we move, we do so decisively and with full assurance as to the outcome. It is when we entertain doubts or allow fear to creep into our thinking that we move with uncertainty. Uncertain actions will reap undesirable fruit.

Our God has promised to support and strengthen our steps as we walk according to His will. He provides us with the confidence and assurance that enable us to fully commit our heart, soul, mind, and strength right from the very first step. He gives us the ability to stand on the heights.

Questions to consider while watching the film:

1. What was it about the dance lessons that so transformed Shohei?

2. Lack of confidence must stem from a condition of fear. What does God say about fear? How can we control it?

Sicko
on
Debt

Film: Sicko (2007)
Directed by: Michael Moore
Written by: Michael Moore
U.S. Distributor: Lionsgate
Starring: Michael Moore
Rated: PG-13

About the film:
Documentary filmmaker Michael Moore turns his cameras onto the broken U.S. health care system to ask the question, "Why does the greatest country in the world have a health care system that cannot provide for the needs of its citizens?"

Movie Quote:
"Choice depends on the freedom to choose and if you are shackled with debt you don't have the freedom to choose."
Tony Benn (as himself) in Sicko (2007)

Bible Quote:
"The rich ruleth over the poor, and the borrower is servant to the lender."
Proverbs 22:7 (KJV)

Commentary:

There is no question that Moore's film shows a dire problem in need of fixing. But tucked away in this scathing attack on for-profit health care is this salient little quote from British politician Tony Benn that speaks volumes about a separate issue. That issue is debt.

The health care debate deserves inspection and discussion, but the debt issue in this country is even more important because it touches upon every single aspect of our lives including our health care. Being in debt restricts our freedom; restricts our choices; restricts our lives. It makes us virtual slaves to those to whom we owe money. And our creditors do not care about us. They only care about what we owe.

And owe we do. In fact, "I owe, I owe, so off to work I go" is the mantra of most Americans. Can we even imagine a scenario that has us working because we want to instead of because we need to? It is hard to imagine because this country not only encourages us to have a debt mentality, it actually adopts one as its own. The unhealthy fiscal practices of our nation make that abundantly clear.

God encourages us to live wisely by living debt-free. Having no debt opens doors of opportunities in all areas of life. These doors have never been closed to us. But how do we expect to walk through them if we have already shackled ourselves to a mountain of debt?

Questions to consider while watching the film:

1. Is there a solution to the U.S. health care crisis? Find scriptural references to support your answer.

2. Why does debt "shackle?" Can debt be used somehow to serve God's purposes?

Solaris
on
Death

Film: Solaris (2002)

Directed by: Steven Soderbergh

Written by: Steven Soderbergh

US Distribution: 20th Century Fox

Starring: George Clooney, Natascha McElhone

Rated: PG-13

About the film:

A troubled psychologist is called to visit the members of a space expedition orbiting the planet Solaris. Upon his arrival, he discovers that strange and unexplained occurrences are threatening their very existence. Oddly enough, the other members of the expedition do not appear to want to discuss it.

Movie Quote:

"And death shall have no dominion."

Chris Kelvin (George Clooney) in Solaris (2002)

Bible Quote:

"Knowing that Christ, being raised from the dead, dieth no more; death hath no more dominion over him."

Romans 6:9 (KJV)

Commentary:

The "Solaris" quote is taken from a Dylan Thomas poem, the title of which is obviously inspired from the scriptures. Every year, when we celebrate Easter in remembrance of Christ's resurrection, these words resonate with eternal significance.

It is impossible to overstate the importance of what God accomplished when He raised Jesus Christ from the dead. Death was defeated. There will be no rematch. The final page of history was written at that moment. It just remains to be played out to its full completion. But we can be assured that there is no longer any uncertainty as to the outcome. We win. Our spiritual adversary loses.

Death holds no dominion over us because it could not hold Jesus Christ in the grave. He was raised from the dead. As we believe in him, our future eternity is assured; our place in heaven is established; and our spiritual rewards are set aside, being stored for us until that glorious day when our Lord returns to gather us together as his church.

Questions to consider while watching the film:

1. The film gives us much to ponder in terms of the differences between reality and perception. Can we ever know what is real or will our perceptions of reality always affect what we experience?

2. It has been said that the spiritual battle between good and evil is fought in the arena of our mind. How is this illustrated in "Solaris"?

The Soloist
on
Loyalty

Film: The Soloist (2009)
Directed by: Joe Wright
Written by: Susannah Grant
U.S. Distributor: Paramount Pictures
Starring: Robert Downey Jr. Jamie Foxx
Rated: PG-13

About the film:
Journalist Steve Lopez discovers a homeless man with a musical gift and works to bring him to the attention of an appreciative world. But the man's mental illness proves to be an obstacle that causes Lopez to reconsider what he is doing and why.

Movie Quote:
"I've learned the dignity of being loyal to something you believe in; of holding onto it, above all else. And above all else, of believing, without question, that it will carry you home."
Steve Lopez (Robert Downey Jr.) in The Soloist (2009)

Bible Quote:
"Fear none of those things which thou shalt suffer: behold, the devil shall cast some of you into prison, that ye may be tried; and ye shall have tribulation ten days: be thou faithful unto death, and I will give thee a crown of life."
Revelation 2:10 (KJV)

Commentary:

Steve Lopez learns a thing or two during his association with Nathaniel, a homeless, mentally ill, and quite talented musician. Being true to something takes effort. At some point along our way, we will all be tempted to take an easy route or make an expedient choice by setting our principles, integrity, or beliefs aside because of stiff opposition.

Being faithful or loyal to one's principles or beliefs brings a certain weight or heft to one's walk. There is a noble, dignified quality that is associated with those who quietly refuse to bow down to or cave in to pressure or tempting pleasures. Our beliefs are what ultimately define us. If we choose only to believe when it is convenient (or when there is no opposition to those beliefs) what are we really saying about ourselves?

Being true to one's beliefs or being faithful and loyal to that which we believe in carries its own reward. It strengthens us, even though we may appear weak. It sustains us, even though we may appear to be failing. It brings us the victory, even though we may appear to be defeated. We must remember that the battles we fight are spiritual ones. And the rewards are eternal.

Questions to consider while watching the film:

1. What did Steve Lopez learn about himself during the course of the film?

2. How can we strengthen our resolve when being tempted to let go of our beliefs due to pressure being applied from outside sources?

Source Code
on
Time

Film: Source Code (2011)

Directed by: Duncan Jones

Written by: Ben Ripley

US Distribution: Summit Entertainment

Starring: Jake Gyllenhaal, Michelle Monaghan

Rated: PG-13

About the film:

A helicopter pilot finds he can relive the last eight minutes of another man's life. He uses this same time period over and over again in order to find the clues needed to discover the identity of a terrorist before that terrorist strikes again.

Movie Quote:

"What would you do if you knew you only had one minute to live?"

"I'd make those seconds count."

Colter (Jake Gyllenhaal) and Christina (Michelle Monaghan) in Source Code (2011)

Bible Quote:

"Redeeming the time, because the days are evil."

Ephesians 5:16 (KJV)

Commentary:

How we spend our time is an individual choice. It is a choice which should be considered very carefully. Time is, after all, the one commodity on earth that cannot be replicated, grown, or hoarded. We cannot make any more of it or store it away for a rainy day. All we can do is to use it in the most effective and meaningful way possible.

Unlike Colter, who has multiple opportunities to relive the same eight minutes to achieve a desired goal, we have just one opportunity to make our seconds count. Once time has passed, there is simply no bringing it back. Therefore, how we spend our time throughout the course of our life will determine whether we look back on it with regret or with satisfaction.

God exhorts us to redeem the time. A literal definition of the word "redeem" is to "rescue from loss." It makes sense because time by itself naturally carries with it a sense of loss. It is what we do with the time we have that gives time purpose and meaning. Make the seconds count. Let life have its purpose.

Questions to consider while watching the film:

1. What does "redeem the time" mean to you? How is it demonstrated in the film?

2. What are the greatest "time stealers" in your life? What can you do to protect yourself against them?

Spider-man
on
Responsibility

Film: Spider-man (2002)
Directed by: Sam Raimi
Written by: David Koepp
U.S. Distributor: Columbia Pictures
Starring: Tobey Maguire, Kirsten Dunst
Rated: PG-13

About the film:

After being bitten by a genetically altered spider, mild-mannered Peter Parker develops superhuman abilities. The world at large begins to distrust him rather than embrace him as a hero. While Parker tries to figure out how to capitalize on his new powers, a second freak accident occurs, turning a scientist into the evil Green Goblin who wreaks havoc upon the town.

Movie Quote:

"With great power comes great responsibility."
Uncle Ben (Cliff Robertson) in Spider-man (2002)

Bible Quote:

"From everyone who has been given much, much will be demanded; and from the one who has been entrusted with much, much more will be asked."
Luke 12:48b (NIV)

Commentary:

Parker's uncle Ben is trying to teach the youthful Peter a lesson that will be vital for him to learn. All men may be equal in the eyes of God, but in terms of abilities, strengths, or long suits, we are not equal. We are individuals with different backgrounds, interests and acquired skills.

As we sojourn in this world, we may find ourselves among a few who excel in a given area. When we do, we should be asking ourselves how we might best use our ability (or power) to its fullest advantage; not for our benefit, but for the benefit of all.

We are called to be part of the body of Christ. As a part of that body, we have a responsibility to use the power we have been given to function in the role to which we have been called. As with our physical body, should one limb or organ fail to perform its function, the whole body suffers as a result.

We have much for which to be thankful. We can express our thankfulness by doing what God would have us do with the power and abilities He has granted us. The body of Christ will be stronger for it.

Questions to consider while watching the film:

1. Prior to the quoted scripture, Jesus tells his disciples a parable. What is the meaning of the parable in context of Luke 12:48 and how does it relate to the film?

2. Peter can be seen as an illustration for a born-again believer. What are the similarities? What are the differences?

Spy Game
on
Preparation

Film: Spy Game (2001)
Directed by: Tony Scott
Written by: Michael Frost Beckner, David Arata
U.S. Distributor: Universal Pictures
Starring: Robert Redford, Brad Pitt
Rated: R

About the film:

One of the last acts a retiring CIA agent must perform is working against his agency superiors to help release his ex-partner from a Chinese prison camp before his execution is carried out. Even as he examines the options available to him, he reflects on his relationship with the man he recruited and trained to be a spy.

Movie Quote:

"When did Noah build the ark Gladys? Before the rain."

Nathan Muir (Robert Redford) in Spy Game (2001)

Bible Quote:

"As it was in the days of Noah, so it will be at the coming of the Son of Man."

 Matthew 24:37 (NIV)

Commentary:

The point Muir is making is that preparation is the key to a successful outcome. God does not want us to fail and so He encourages us to learn from the past, live for today, and plan for tomorrow.

Had Noah waited for the first raindrop before starting to build the ark, the world today would be ruled by fish. The key to his (and our) survival was his obedience to prepare for the rain he did not see coming.

We, like Noah, have been given an opportunity to escape a future calamity. But if we wait until it arrives before we choose to take action, we will miss the boat and be left behind. God has given us a way to avoid the tribulation that is to come.

When Jesus Christ returns, he is coming for his church. All born-again believers will be removed from this earth and taken to our new spiritual home which he has prepared for us. We are exhorted to prepare for his future arrival by believing today. The instruction in Romans 10:9 explains to us what we are to believe. All that remains is for us to follow that instruction and then continue living our lives with the newly acquired hope of salvation in our hearts.

Questions to consider while watching the film:

1. Why did Muir break his own rules that he once said were inviolate in order to save Bishop?

2. What are the moral dangers in viewing the world as Muir views it; where people, places, and things are all considered to be assets that can be used and discarded for the purpose of the mission?

Star Trek
on
Dual Citizenship

Film: Star Trek (2009)
Directed by: J.J. Abrams
Written by: Roberto Orci, Alex Kurtzman
U.S. Distributor: Paramount Pictures
Starring: Chris Pine, Zachary Quinto
Rated: PG-13

About the film:

"Star Trek" cleverly reinvents itself and breathes new life into a familiar franchise. The origins of Kirk, Spock, Scotty and the rest of the crew of the USS Enterprise are explored and explained as they once again find themselves on a mission to save the universe.

Movie Quote:

"You will always be a child of two worlds, and fully capable of deciding your own destiny. The question you face is: which path will you choose?"
Sarek (Ben Cross) in Star Trek (2009)

Bible Quote:

"That which is born of the flesh is flesh; and that which is born of the Spirit is spirit."
John 3:6 (KJV)

Commentary:

The unique Vulcan/Earth lineage of "Star Trek's" Mr. Spock, which had him constantly warring within himself, was what made him such a compelling and popular figure. But perhaps it was not all that unique. Are we not all children of two worlds?

On the one hand, we are the children of our mother and father and are raised in a world with physical rules and laws which are ingrained in us from birth. On the other hand, we are also children of our heavenly Father and are granted spiritual life that has its own set of rules and laws which we can learn about through study of God's Word.

We live in this world but, as God reminds us in Philippians 3:20, our citizenship is in heaven. We must learn, as Spock did, how to control certain tendencies which are attributed to our natural or earthly manner in order to adopt the higher spiritual qualities appropriate to God's children and His ambassadors while on earth.

Walking by the flesh or walking by the spirit? It is a fundamental daily choice that we all have to make. The thing to remember is that only one of those choices carries with it eternal rewards.

Questions to consider while watching the film:

1. What leadership qualities did Kirk have that made him the right person to sit in the captain's chair?

2. If your future self could visit you today, what advice do you think he or she would have?

Star Trek II
on
Longevity

Film: Star Trek II (1982)

Directed by: Nicholas Meyer

Written by: Jack B. Sowards

U.S. Distributor: Paramount Pictures

Starring: William Shatner, Leonard Nimoy

Rated: PG

About the film:

Captain Kirk, beginning to feel the effects of his age, gets a surprise as his old nemesis, Khan, returns with an aim to exact his revenge. Kirk gathers the old crew of the Enterprise and once again goes where no man has gone before in an attempt to stop Khan's threat and save the Federation.

Movie Quote:

"Live long and prosper."

Spock (Leonard Nimoy) in Star Trek II (1982)

Bible Quote:

"Beloved, I wish above all things that thou mayest prosper and be in health, even as thy soul prospereth."

3 John 1:2 (KJV)

Commentary:

Who knew that Mr. Spock's classic line from "Star Trek" had biblical roots? Indeed, this is God's greatest desire. His passionate will above everything else is for His beloved children to prosper and be in health as we live long and fruitful lives.

Throughout His Word, God gives us instruction on how we might achieve such a desired result. In Ephesians 6:2-3 we read, "Honor your father and mother" (which is the first commandment with a promise) "that it may go well with you and that you may enjoy long life on the earth." God cannot say something if it is not true. A long and happy life is a reward of obedience.

As far as prosperity is concerned, 2 Corinthians 9:6 holds a fundamental principle of a life that is more than abundant: "Remember this: Whoever sows sparingly will also reap sparingly, and whoever sows generously will also reap generously." God promises that as we give we shall receive. It is one of three spiritual keys to financial prosperity: Work heartily as to the Lord; live within one's means; and share abundantly.

Live long and prosper. It is more than a catch phrase. It is God's heartfelt desire for our lives.

Questions to consider while watching the film:

1. If it is God's will that we prosper, why do many Christians suffer from financial difficulties?

2. Is the line "the needs of the many outweigh the needs of the few" an accurate spiritual belief? Why or why not?

Star Trek VI
on
Logic

Film: Star Trek VI (1991)
Directed by: Nicholas Meyer
Written by: Nicholas Meyer, Denny Martin Flinn
U.S. Distributor: Paramount Pictures
Starring: William Shatner, Leonard Nimoy
Rated: PG

About the film:
The Klingon Empire and the Federation are on the verge of signing a peace treaty which will end generations of conflict and warfare. But someone is out to sabotage the accord and the crew of the Enterprise must take action to prevent them from succeeding.

Movie Quote:
"Logic, logic, logic. Logic is the beginning of wisdom, Valeris, not the end."
Spock (Leonard Nimoy) in Star Trek VI (1991)

Bible Quote:
"The fear (respect or reverence) of the LORD is the beginning of wisdom; all who follow His precepts have good understanding."
Psalms 111:10 (NIV)

Commentary:

Spock says that logic is the beginning of wisdom. Scripture says that having respect or reverence towards God is the beginning of wisdom. Oddly enough, we do not really have to choose between the two. The key to understanding how these quotes complement each other can be found in the opening verse of the gospel of John: "In the beginning was the Word (logos), and the Word (logos) was with God, and the Word (logos) was God." John 1:1 (NIV)

The Greek word logos, which is obviously related to the English word for logic, is used in the scriptures to refer not only to God but also God's will, God's son who always did His will, as well as the written Word which was given by God to reveal His will.

Believing in God's Word is inherently "logical." As we apply that logic or sound and rational thinking to our lives, we gain wisdom. But as Spock notes, logic is only the beginning. And wisdom is not the end. As we faithfully act with wisdom, over time we will gain something even greater: understanding. We are given the ability to see the big picture. We will mentally see how all the pieces of knowledge and wisdom fit together to form the grand tapestry of the life which God designed.

Questions to consider while watching the film:

1. If respect or reverence to God equals logic, where does illogical thinking come from?

2. The peace talks between the Klingons and the Federation are being threatened by an unseen opponent. The peace in our hearts is often similarly disrupted. How might we counter that which prevents us from being at peace?

Star Wars
on
God

Film: Star Wars (1977)
Directed by: George Lucas
Written by: George Lucas
U.S. Distributor: 20th Century Fox
Starring: Mark Hamill, Harrison Ford, Carrie Fisher
Rated: PG

About the film:
A young farm boy is swept into an intergalactic adventure as he teams with a renegade space smuggler and a pair of androids to rescue Princess Leia who has been taken captive by the Imperial Forces. Once the princess is safe, they must then defend the galaxy against the evil invaders.

Movie Quote:
"The Force will be with you... always."
Ben Obi-Wan Kenobi (Alec Guinness) in Star Wars (1977)

Bible Quote:
"The LORD himself goes before you and will be with you; he will never leave you nor forsake you. Do not be afraid; do not be discouraged."
Deuteronomy 31:8 (NIV)

Commentary:

Obi-Wan offers words of encouragement to the young untested farm boy who will eventually become a great Jedi knight. How does "The Force" of which he speaks relate to our lives?

The word that leaps out in the quoted phrase from the movie is "always." We hear that word so often being used by men who eventually disappoint us that perhaps it has lost some of its impact. The word literally means "at all times" or "in every instance." When referring to the presence of God in our lives, it is a word that carries great import.

God is always with us. No matter where we go, He is with us. Every time we turn to Him, He is there. Every time we speak to Him, He hears us. He walks before us, showing us the way. He walks beside us, giving us strength. He walks behind us, supporting us and encouraging us to continue. Most importantly, He dwells within us, filling us with His love and His strength and His power.

His promise to us is that He will never leave us nor forsake us. It is a promise that He has always kept to those people who love Him. Always.

Questions to consider while watching the film:

1. How does Luke's struggle to trust and use "The Force" compare to our learning how to trust and use the power of holy spirit?

2. Han Solo undergoes a radical change of character during the course of the film. Why? What does that say about how our lives might affect our unbelieving friends and family members?

Star Wars: Episode V
on
Appearances

Film: Star Wars: Episode V (1980)
Directed by: Irvin Kershner
Written by: Leigh Brackett, Lawrence Kasdan
U.S. Distributor: 20th Century Fox
Starring: Mark Hamill, Harrison Ford, Carrie Fisher
Rated: PG

About the film:

In this continuation of the "Star Wars" saga, Luke receives advanced Jedi training from Jedi master Yoda. Meanwhile, his friends are captured by Darth Vader which means that Luke must quickly utilize all he has learned in order to rescue them.

Movie Quote:

"Size matters not. Look at me. Judge me by my size, do you? Hmm? Hmm? And well you should not. For my ally is the Force, and a powerful ally it is."
Yoda (Frank Oz) in Star Wars: Episode V (1980)

Bible Quote:

"You, dear children, are from God and have overcome them, because the one who is in you is greater than the one who is in the world."
1 John 4:4 (NIV)

Commentary:

It is hard to imagine that the muppet-like Yoda would be capable of accomplishing any great physical feat. It is because we have become accustomed to sizing things up and reaching conclusions based solely upon our natural man or sense knowledge awareness. As Yoda so quickly points out, this would be a serious misjudgment on our part.

Bigger is not necessarily better. In fact, where God is concerned, size is of no consequence. God's strength and might can work within even the smallest individual and bring victory to a situation despite overwhelming odds or resistance.

Because of his believing, David defeated Goliath even though he was at a great physical disadvantage. Because of his believing, Gideon and 300 unarmed men conquered an army of Midianites. Because of his believing, Moses stood in front of the vast Red Sea and, calling upon the power of God, commanded the sea itself to part.

The various obstacles and adversities that we face in life may appear to us to be unbeatable if we look at them at face value. What we must remember is that we do not tackle our problems alone. As we believe and trust in God, there is no enemy that we cannot drive back and no obstacle that we cannot overcome.

Questions to consider while watching the film:

1. What should be the criteria used when estimating a person's worth or value to us?

2. What must Yoda teach Luke before he can grow in his knowledge and understanding of "The Force"? What are the spiritual implications of this?

Starman
on
Adversity

Film: Starman (1984)
Directed by: John Carpenter
Written by: Bruce A. Evans, Raynold Gideon
U.S. Distributor: Columbia Pictures
Starring: Jeff Bridges, Karen Allen
Rated: PG

About the film:
When an alien crashes and becomes stranded on Earth, he takes the form of a young widow's late husband and requests that she drive him across the country to a predetermined extraction point. Government agents hotly pursue the couple, wanting to study the alien more closely.

Movie Quote:
"Shall I tell you what I find beautiful about you? You are at your very best when things are worst."
Starman (Jeff Bridges) in Starman (1980)

Bible Quote:
"No, in all these things we are more than conquerors through him who loved us."
Romans 8:37 (NIV)

Commentary:

The alien in "Starman" makes an interesting observation based upon watching how humans act and react to various situations. From his perspective it may seem a bit incongruous that, as things around us get bad, we tend to rise to the occasion and get better.

His observation brings to mind the phrase, "The darker it gets, the brighter the light can shine." It is impossible for darkness to extinguish light. All it can do is make it more noticeable.

Leading up to Romans 8:37, the apostle Paul lists a series of cataclysmic events (persecution, famine, peril, sword, etc.) in order to make the point that, despite what our outward circumstances may be, our inner strength will be sufficient to overcome them. The reason for this is because our inner strength comes from God whose power knows no equal.

The more we draw upon God's strength and power, the more we will prevail over the many obstacles we face in our lives. The more we prevail in the face of overwhelming odds, the brighter our lives will shine; reflecting His light for the entire world to see.

Questions to consider while watching the film:

1. Why does Jenny change her mind and begin to help the alien? What does the Bible say about giving aid to strangers in need?

2. Why does the alien take on the appearance of Jenny's dead husband? What can we learn from that as we approach people with the good news of Christ?

Sunshine
on
Light

Film: Sunshine (2007)
Directed by: Danny Boyle
Written by: Alex Garland
U.S. Distributor: Fox Searchlight
Starring: Chris Evans, Rose Byrnes, Michelle Yeoh
Rated: R

About the film:
When the sun begins to burn out, Earth's scientists send a team armed with a massive nuclear device who will attempt to detonate it within the heart of the star and thus reignite it. The journey is rife with problems which lead to moral and ethical dilemmas.

Movie Quote:
"You and the darkness are distinct from each other because darkness is an absence of something, it's a vacuum. But total light envelops you. It becomes you."
Dr. Searle (Cliff Curtis) in Sunshine (2007)

Bible Quote:
"And the Light shines on in the darkness, for the darkness has never overpowered it [put it out or absorbed it or appropriated it, and is unreceptive to it]."
John 1:5 (Amplified)

Commentary:

Dr. Searle's fascination with light is one that we can share. For those who have been long immersed in darkness, the introduction of light equates to deliverance and salvation. His observation is also astute. Darkness is nothing more than the absence of light. They cannot co-mingle. Once light is introduced, darkness immediately ceases.

Because this is so evidently true in the physical world, is it no wonder that God uses light as a figurative means to describe spiritual awareness or understanding? People who live without knowledge of God and the spiritual truths He has set in place are said to be living in darkness. It is His Word, set in the stars, handed down through generations, recorded in the Bible, or taught and witnessed through the life of Jesus Christ, which has reached into the darkness and illuminated the hearts of men.

We can never be at one with the darkness for darkness blinds us and keeps us in ignorance. We can however be at one with light. We can allow it to infuse our being and continue to shine forth through our words and action. We can be, indeed we are in God's mind, the lights of this world.

Questions to consider while watching the film:

1. What are some of the ethical questions that face the crew of the Icarus II and how biblically sound are their responses?

2. When one of the characters in the film states that he has spoken to God, is he speaking truth or a lie? How do we know?

Sunshine
on
Ego

Film: Sunshine (1999)
Directed by: István Szabó
Written by: István Szabó, Israel Horovitz
U.S. Distributor: Paramount Classics
Starring: Ralph Fiennes, Rosemary Harris
Rated: R

About the film:

"Sunshine" follows the trials and tribulations of three generations of the Sonnenschein family. The film spans over seventy years of European history as it tracks this family of Hungarian Jews who live through two world wars and a seemingly endless parade of governments and philosophies.

Movie Quote:

"Never allow yourself to be driven into the sin of conceit. Conceit is the greatest of sins. The source of all other sins."

Ignatz Sonnenschein (Ralph Fiennes) in Sunshine (1999)

Bible Quote:

"For whoever exalts himself will be humbled, and whoever humbles himself will be exalted."

Luke 14:11 (NIV)

Commentary:

Ego or conceit can be a stumbling block to one's personal growth and development, especially if it runs unchecked and uncontrolled. Ego can lead a person to make decisions and take actions that will produce far less than that which is desired. Scripture even states that it was ego that led to the first recorded sin of all time. That sin, of course, was Lucifer's betrayal.

A simple definition of "sin" might be rendered "broken fellowship with God." When we sin, we are choosing to do something contrary to God's expressed will for our lives. We walk away from Him, choosing instead our own way rather than God's way. We are, in effect, saying that we know more about how to live our lives than the God who created them. Is that not the height of ego?

An ego-driven step will always be a step in the wrong direction. Humility may be a much maligned or neglected quality in this world but it is still held in high esteem by the one judge who truly matters. A humble spirit will always be rewarded beyond measure.

Questions to consider while watching the film:

1. Can it be said that conceit is the source of all other sins? In what way?

2. What are some examples of meekness and humility that are recorded in the Bible and what results did those who displayed those qualities receive?

Talk Radio
on
Words

Film: Talk Radio (1988)
Directed by: Oliver Stone
Written by: Eric Bogosian, Oliver Stone
U.S. Distributor: Universal Pictures
Starring: Eric Bogosian, Ellen Green, Alec Baldwin
Rated: R

About the film:
Barry Champlain, an abrasive and controversial talk show radio host who has made a career out of insulting his callers, is about to break into national syndication. But before he does he must deal with executives who want him to tone down his blistering rhetoric while handling the death threats that continue to stream into the studio from the neo-Nazi groups he has offended.

Movie Quote:
"Sticks and stones can hurt my bones but words cause permanent damage!"
Barry (Eric Bogosian) in Talk Radio (1988)

Bible Quote:
"All kinds of animals, birds, reptiles and creatures of the sea are being tamed and have been tamed by man; but no man can tame the tongue. It is a restless evil, full of deadly poison."
James 3:7-8 (NIV)

Commentary:

Of all the harm that man can inflict upon one another, the injuries that take the longest to heal are the ones caused by the impact of the words we speak.

The central character of "Talk Radio" makes his living by releasing the power of his words across the nation's airwaves without thought or consideration as to the impact or effect they will have upon those who hear them. Such blatant disregard for one's fellow man is unconscionable. And yet it is difficult to point a finger of blame without turning it upon ourselves as well.

Why is it then that we are so unaware of the power that is unleashed with every utterance we make? Words constantly leave our lips with thoughtless abandon. They become random "fiery darts" that will ultimately find a target and leave their mark.

It does not have to be so. All it takes is a bit of deliberation and a desire to bless instead of blast. Words can be used to comfort, edify and heal. It is entirely up to us as to how we employ them.

"Reckless words pierce like a sword, but the tongue of the wise brings healing." Proverbs 12:18 (NIV)

Questions to consider while watching the film:

1. How do we balance man's right to freedom of speech with God's exhortation to speak only words of grace and edification?

2. How much of today's talk radio is exploitation? Where do we draw the boundaries between entertainment, information, and propaganda?

Thirteen Conversations
About One Thing
on
Luck

Film: Thirteen Conversations About One Thing (2001)
Directed by: Jill Sprecher
Written by: Karen Sprecher, Jill Sprecher
U.S. Distributor: Sony Pictures Classics
Starring: Matthew McConaughey, Alan Arkin
Rated: R

About the film:
The "one thing" referenced in the title of the film is happiness. More importantly, the question the film asks is, "How does one achieve happiness in life?"

Movie Quote:
"Luck is the lazy man's excuse."
Troy (Matthew McConaughey) in Thirteen Conversations About One Thing (2001)

Bible Quote:
"But the man who looks intently into the perfect law that gives freedom, and continues to do this, not forgetting what he has heard, but doing it – he will be blessed in what he does."
James 1:25 (NIV)

MICHAEL ELLIOTT

Commentary:

Luck and fate are concepts created by man to try to explain why things happen the way they happen. Those who put their trust in such things are bound to be disappointed because they fail to see that God, when He created the universe, designed it purposefully. It functions by a set of laws and standards.

Whenever we think about "luck," we should remember the words of Thomas Jefferson who purportedly said, "I'm a great believer in luck and I find the harder I work, the more I have of it."

To believe in luck is "a lazy man's excuse" because it relinquishes us of responsibility. It indicates a belief that no action on our part will change what "luck" will bring us. This is about as non-scriptural a mindset that we could possibly have.

God did not establish a "law of luck." He did establish the "law of believing." As we believe according to His will and take actions that are aligned with our believing, He promises that we shall receive that which we desire.

God does not want us to be lucky. He wants us to be blessed.

Questions to consider while watching the film:

1. Where does "bad luck" come from? How can it be avoided?

2. Of the characters in the film, which ones demonstrate the most positive characteristics that we would want to emulate in our lives? Why?

174

Thirteen Days
on
Men of Good Will

Film: Thirteen Days (2000)
Directed by: Roger Donaldson
Written by: David Self
U.S. Distributor: New Line Cinema
Starring: Kevin Costner, Bruce Greenwood
Rated: PG-13

About the film:
The Kennedy administration must deal with the growing threat of Russian missiles being placed in Cuba, knowing that they are capable of striking the United States. All the political rhetoric does not mask the very real tension which will be felt during these next thirteen days as the world balances precariously on the brink of a major military standoff between two superpowers.

Movie Quote:
"If the sun comes up tomorrow, it is only because of men of good will. That is all there is between us and the devil." Kenny O'Donnell (Kevin Costner) in Thirteen Days (2000)

Bible Quote:
"So he said he would destroy them – had not Moses, his chosen one, stood in the breach before him to keep his wrath from destroying them."
Psalms 106:23 (NIV)

175

Commentary:

Throughout history, there have been men who were asked to rise to an occasion and make decisions or take actions that would affect countless others. At such times, it would be comforting to know that these leaders trust in and rely upon the power and wisdom of God to guide them.

How important is it that men continue to believe and manifest the power of God in this world? Where would the world be if Moses had chosen not to return to Egypt to lead God's chosen people to the Promised Land? Or if Noah had allowed himself to be tainted by the corrupt and perverse times in which he lived? What if David took one look at Goliath and ran in the opposite direction?

The courageous, believing stand of one man or one woman is often all that stood between victory and defeat of an entire people. We, above all others, have cause to appreciate this truth. It is through the life of one man that we have received our spiritual deliverance.

For as long as we continue to live in this world, we can be those "men of good will" who stand in the breach. With Jesus Christ as our example, our lives can be as shining lights able to hold the spiritual darkness at bay.

Questions to consider while watching the film:

1. Scripture says that there is "safety in a multitude of counselors." How does this film illustrate that truth?

2. The film addresses the fact that many times a character did not feel worthy or equipped to do the job he was being asked to do. What should we do when we feel the same way?

Time Bandits
on
Evil

Film: Time Bandits (1981)
Directed by: Terry Gilliam
Written by: Terry Gilliam, Michael Palin
U.S. Distributor: AVCO Embassy Pictures
Starring: David Rappaport, Kenny Baker
Rated: PG

About the film:
A young boy joins a band of dwarves on a time-traveling adventure. The dwarves have stolen a map showing the location of "time holes" from The Supreme Being which allows them to escape through time so they can plunder to their heart's content.

Movie Quote:
"No one created me! I am Evil! Evil existed long before Good. I cannot be unmade. I am all-powerful."
Evil Genius (David Warner) in Time Bandits (1981)

Bible Quote:
"I form the light, and create darkness; I make peace, and created evil: I the LORD do all these things."
Isaiah 45:7 (KJV)

Commentary:

The number of lies contained in this one quote attributed to Evil Genius is mind-boggling. Contrary to his claims, evil is not all-powerful. It can be "unmade." It did not exist before good. And as the scripture from Isaiah informs us, evil was purposely created. It was created by none other than God Himself.

That may seem a bit contradictory and even blasphemous to say but because the Word of God declares it to be true, we must accept it and try to understand what it means. As we delve deeper into the nature of God we find that it is not contradictory at all.

Evil exists because we have a kind, fair, just and loving God. We have a God who did not want His people to be mindless robots or puppets which could be controlled by the pulling of a string. He had to create the possibility of both good and evil so He could then grant us the free will to choose between the two.

The ultimate expression of love that we can give to our Creator and our God is found in our faithfulness to always choose good, thus fulfilling His greatest joy.

"I have no greater joy than to hear that my children are walking in the truth." 3 John 1:4 (NIV)

Questions to consider while watching the film:

1. Would you choose to give up your free will in order to live in a world without evil? Why or why not?

2. How does Romans 12:21 apply to this film?

Tombstone
on
Stars

Film: Tombstone (1993)
Directed by: George P. Cosmatos
Written by: Kevin Jarre
U.S. Distributor: Buena Vista Pictures
Starring: Kurt Russell, Val Kilmer, Sam Elliott
Rated: R

About the film:

Wyatt Earp moves to Tombstone, Arizona with his brothers and his old friend Doc Holliday. His plans for a peaceful retirement from law enforcement are interrupted by a group of outlaws who call themselves The Cowboys.

Movie Quote:

"Look at all the stars. You look up and you think, 'God made all this and He remembered to make a little speck like me.' It's kind of flattering, really."

Morgan Earp (Bill Paxton) in Tombstone (1993)

Bible Quote:

"When I consider your heavens, the work of your fingers, the moon and the stars, which you have set in place, what is man that you are mindful of him, the son of man that you care for him?"

Psalms 8:3-4 (NIV)

Commentary:

As we can see from the scriptures, Morgan Earp was not the first one to look at the creation of God with awe and wonder. How much more "flattered" might Morgan have been to know that we were not just one of God's afterthoughts but the reason behind creation itself?

At the center of God's heart has always been the desire to have a family. He wants to enjoy fellowship. He wants to love and be loved in return. We are the recipients of that love. All that was made by Him was made with us in mind.

The heavens were positioned precisely so that human life could be sustained on this planet. The earth was created so that it could nutritionally support life and aesthetically please and bless us. No other planet in the universe provides us with all our needs the way the earth does. God designed it for us.

The psalmist asks a question that, at the time he wrote it, was not able to be answered fully. It is now, because of what the sacrifice of Jesus Christ made available. What is man, that God is mindful of him? For those who believe, the answer is obvious. We are His children.

Questions to consider while watching the film:

1. Compare and contrast the motivations of the various characters (notably Wyatt Earp, Doc Holliday, Curly Bill and Johnny Ringo.)

2. Why did Virgil Earp decide to accept the sheriff's badge? What is our obligation when we find ourselves confronted with injustice?

Top Gun
on
Self-Improvement

Film: Top Gun (1986)
Directed by: Tony Scott
Written by: Jim Cash, Jack Epps Jr.
U.S. Distributor: Paramount Pictures
Starring: Tom Cruise, Kelly McGillis
Rated: PG

About the film:
The best pilots of the U.S. Navy compete for the honor of being "top gun." Maverick is one of the leading contenders until a tragedy causes him to lose his nerve. With support from his commanding officer and the love of an attractive Top Gun instructor, Maverick struggles to regain his confidence.

Movie Quote:
"A good pilot always evaluates what's happened so he can apply what he's learned."
Viper (Tom Skerritt) in Top Gun (1986)

Bible Quote:
"Anyone who listens to the Word but does not do what it says is like a man who looks at his face in a mirror and, after looking at himself, goes away and immediately forgets what he looks like."
James 1:23-24 (NIV)

Commentary:

We can use all of life's experiences, good or bad, to better ourselves. If we treat each experience as a time of learning and evaluation, we can grow and mature on a daily basis. Every experience is like a snapshot that allows us to look in a mirror and see where we are in terms of our development.

Mirrors grant us the ability to examine ourselves as we actually are. If we do not like what we see in the reflection (i.e., a hair out of place, a blemish, etc.), we have the opportunity to correct it before we present ourselves to the rest of the world.

The Word of God also shows us a reflection. It is a reflection of what we can be. If we do not recognize ourselves in His Word, we then have the opportunity to make changes in our lives so we might more closely match the vision God has for us.

The Word, like a mirror, will only work if we take the time and expend the energy to study what is there, evaluate the reflection and take corrective action based upon what we see. If we do not like what we see of ourselves in God's Word, but we take no action to change, we have no one to blame but ourselves when we fail to receive all that God says He is willing to give us.

Questions to consider while watching the film:

1. What lessons did Maverick learn during the course of the film and how do they equate with biblical lessons addressed to us?

2. The quoted verse of scripture indicates that if we do not apply what we learn, we will forget it. What examples of this can you think of either from the Bible or from your own experience?

182

Toy Story 3
on
Faithfulness

Film: Toy Story 3 (2010)
Directed by: Lee Unkrich
Written by: Michael Arndt
U.S. Distributor: Walt Disney Studios
Starring: Tom Hanks, Tim Allen, Joan Cusack
Rated: G

About the film:
The third film of the series finds Andy destined for
college and his lifelong toys awaiting the decision as to
their fate. As the toys embark on what may be their final
adventure, the movie pulls a few heartstrings with its
message of friendship, loyalty, and lessons learned.

Movie Quote:
"Now Woody, he's been my pal for as long as I can
remember. He's brave, like a cowboy should be, and kind,
and smart. But the thing that makes Woody special is he'll
never give up on you... ever. He'll be there for you, no
matter what."
Andy (John Morris) in Toy Story 3 (2010)

Bible Quote:
"Have I not commanded you? Be strong and courageous.
Do not be afraid; do not be discouraged, for the LORD
your God will be with you wherever you go."
Joshua 1:9 (NIV)

MICHAEL ELLIOTT

Commentary:

The qualities used to describe the characteristics of a fictional toy cowboy speak of an ideal. It is an ideal that is not often realized in the world in which we live. But it is an ideal most of us crave. We yearn to have a friend in whom we can trust implicitly, without reservation, because he never disappoints us.

Woody, an imaginary friend, was that to Andy. And the imaginary bond that was formed between the toy and the boy helped the child develop into a caring, sensitive young man. Who would not want to have a friend like Woody?

The truth is that we have it better. We have, not just a friend, but a father. We have a father who is incapable of lying, cheating, or disappointing. We have a father who will never leave us in our times of need nor forsake us when we are at our weakest. We have a father who patiently waits for us to come to the realization that He loves us and will do anything for us. He will not give up on us ever. He will always be there for us, no matter what.

Questions to consider while watching the film:

1. What responsibilities do we have to those who have influenced our lives?

2. What is the goal of the toys of "Toy Story 3"? How does that equate to the goals we set for ourselves? Are the goals we set ones that enable us to serve or ones that will position us to be served? Which is better?

Troy
on
War

Film: Troy (2004)
Directed by: Wolfgang Petersen
Written by: David Benioff
U.S. Distributor: Warner Brothers
Starring: Brad Pitt, Eric Bana, Orlando Bloom
Rated: R

About the film:
A non-mythical telling of the Trojan War, the film begins with Paris, the younger prince of Troy, stealing the wife of the Spartan king. The king turns to his brother Agamemnon for help to restore his honor by waging war against Troy.

Movie Quote:
"I've fought many wars in my time. Some I've fought for land, some for power, some for glory. I suppose fighting for love makes more sense than all the rest."
Priam, king of Troy (Peter O'Toole) in Troy (2004)

Bible Quote:
"From whence comes wars and fighting among you? Come they not hence, even of your lusts that war in your members?"
James 4:1 (KJV)

Commentary:

From his quote, we see that Priam is looking to rationalize what he knows will be a bloody and deadly conflict. The love he has for his son causes him to try and justify the war he knows will follow. But he is wrong.

What is the likelihood that, when we finally reach our heavenly home and look back upon our history, there will be much recorded about man's justifications for the wars that were fought?

God has already revealed to us about wars and why they happen. It has nothing to do with glory or honor or love. Wars occur because of our own weaknesses, fears, and frailties. They occur because the human race, as a whole, too often fails to travel the path along which our God has directed us to follow.

Because we live in this world, we must deal with the reality of this world. Sadly, wars will continue to be waged as long as we are upon this earth. God tells us not to be terrified by this. Instead, He tells us to live with the hope and understanding that a day is coming when a new world will exist. It will be a world without war. It will be a world without sorrow. It will be a world worth waiting for.

Questions to consider while watching the film:

1. Why did the legendary Greek warrior Achilles choose to sail to Troy and fight alongside Agamemnon's army? Why was it important to him? Contrast his reasons for fighting with the reasons of Hector (older brother of Paris).

2. How could this war have been avoided? What actions could have been taken (or not taken) by the characters to prevent the tragedy that followed?

Tuck Everlasting
on
Death

Film: Tuck Everlasting (2002)
Directed by: Jay Russell
Written by: Jeffrey Lieber, James V. Hart
U.S. Distributor: Buena Vista Pictures
Starring: Alexis Bledel, William Hurt, Sissy Spacek
Rated: PG

About the film:

Winnie Foster is a young woman who meets the Tuck family and discovers that they never age. The Tucks offer her the secret to their immortality. All she must do is drink from a spring which serves as a fountain of youth. But, they caution, such a decision is not to be made lightly.

Movie Quote:

"Do not be afraid of death Winnie; be afraid of the unlived life."
Angus Tuck (William Hurt) in Tuck Everlasting (2002)

Bible Quote:

"He too shared in their humanity so that by his death he might destroy him who holds the power of death – that is, the devil – and free those who all their lives were held in slavery by their fear of death."
Hebrews 2:14b-15 (NIV)

Commentary:

Immortality is something that most of us have thought about at one time or another. That thought or desire, when evidenced in a film's character, usually stems from that character's fear of dying. It is a fear that is common to man.

Even though a fear of death may be something we have all experienced, if we take the time to actually consider it, we will realize that holding such a fear is irrational. Death is inevitable and will come to us all. Only the arrival of the Lord will prevent it and the timing of that event is not within our control.

If we choose to live our lives fearing death, we will actually prevent ourselves from living a full and fulfilling life. Fear is an inhibitor. It builds a barrier around those it controls and binds them within, hindering them from achieving their desires and goals.

Only by being delivered from a fear of death may we truly embrace and appreciate all that this life has to offer. Such deliverance is available due to the sacrifice of Jesus Christ. The eternal life which he promises is not based in fear. It is a reality born of love.

Questions to consider while watching the film:

1. If a spring really did exist that would give eternal life in this world to anyone who drank from it, would you drink? Why or why not?

2. What were the reasons Winnie had for her decision? Do you think she had regrets?

The Ultimate Gift
on
Self-Discipline

Film: The Ultimate Gift (2006)
Directed by: Michael O. Sajbel
Written by: Cheryl McKay
U.S. Distributor: FoxFaith
Starring: Drew Fuller, Abigail Breslin, James Garner
Rated: PG

About the film:
A spoiled young man inherits not the riches he expected, but the keys to riches he never before dreamed were possible. He is just slow to realize the unique opportunity that has been gifted to him.

Movie Quote:
"Any process worth going through will get tougher before it gets easier. That's what makes learning a gift, even though pain is your teacher."
"Red" Stevens (James Gardner) in The Ultimate Gift (2006)

Bible Quote:
"No discipline seems pleasant at the time, but painful. Later on, however, it produces a harvest of righteousness and peace for those who have been trained by it."
Hebrews 12:11 (NIV)

Commentary:

What a tremendous life lesson (or series of lessons) that Red Stevens bestows upon his grandson Jason. Many parents make the natural and understandable mistake of providing not only for their children's needs but also for most of their wants. The mistake is born out of a genuine love for the child. But what is lost is the character building that comes with self-discipline, patience, and restraint that are required when children are instead encouraged to work towards achieving the goals they desire.

These are lessons that God teaches His children. While it is true that He has given us all things, it only means that all things are available to us. His abundance is ours as we discipline our lives and conduct ourselves according to His will. He gives to us freely but He also desires that we freely renew our minds and frame our actions to the truths and principles of His Word. When we do, His blessings are showered upon us.

Of course, this is easier said than done. Disciplining one's self requires the willingness to change. And change can be hard. But as the scripture indicates, it has rewards later on. Change can be painful. But that pain is momentary and transitory. As we break through our bad habits and old man natures, we discover a truth and a way of life that so restores our souls that we have neither the time nor inclination to reflect on what we had to do to receive it.

Questions to consider while watching the film:

1. What is the "ultimate gift" and why?

2. Consider each "lesson" that Jason receives. What scriptures come to mind with each lesson?

The Untouchables
on
Perseverance

Film: The Untouchables (1987)
Directed by: Brian De Palma
Written by: David Mamet
U.S. Distributor: Paramount Pictures
Starring: Kevin Costner, Sean Connery
Rated: R

About the film:

As Al Capone rises to power in the Prohibition Era Chicago underworld, federal agent Eliot Ness makes plans to end his criminal reign by adopting unorthodox methods. Unable to trust the system which has been corrupted by Capone's graft, Ness decides to operate independently, using only a small band of men which includes a veteran cop, a rookie, and an accountant to bring the fight to Capone's crime syndicate.

Movie Quote:

"Never stop, never stop fighting till the fight is done."
Eliot Ness (Kevin Costner) in The Untouchables (1987)

Bible Quote:

"I have fought the good fight, I have finished the race, I have kept the faith."
2 Timothy 4:7 (NIV)

Commentary:

In a heavyweight bout, it is rather obvious what would happen if one boxer stopped fighting while his opponent continued. The technical term is called a "knockout." Spiritually, the same misguided action would most certainly bring about the same disastrous result.

We can often forget we are in a spiritual fight because our adversary does not like to face us "toe to toe." He is a sneaky fighter, preferring to circle around behind us and throw "sucker punches" when we are not looking. Fighting a "good fight of faith" (1 Timothy 6:12) requires daily diligence against an unseen and dirty opponent.

We, ourselves, will never land a knockout blow against our adversary. For us, the fight does not end until the final bell rings (or trumpet sounds). It is then that the true champion will reenter the ring and end this fight once and for all. Until then, we are to keep our guard up and our believing strong, to hold our spiritual opponent at bay.

Questions to consider while watching the film:

1. At the end of the film Ness says, "I have broken every law I swore to defend. I have become what I beheld and I am content that I have done right." Was Ness justified in taking the action he did? Why or why not?

2. The film's title refers to the four men who aim to bring Capone to justice. Why were they "untouchable?"

The Usual Suspects
on
The Devil

Film: The Usual Suspects (1987)
Directed by: Bryan Singer
Written by: Christopher McQuarrie
U.S. Distributor: Gramercy Pictures
Starring: Kevin Spacey, Benicio Del Toro,
Rated: R

About the film:
During a routine investigation, police decide to gather up five known criminals for questioning. While in the holding pen, the five conspire to do a job together. That job will put them on the radar of a legendary criminal mastermind known as Keyser Soze, whose name strikes fear in even the most hardened of felons.

Movie Quote:
"The greatest trick the devil ever pulled was convincing the world he didn't exist."
Verbal Kint (Kevin Spacey) in The Usual Suspects (1995)

Bible Quote:
"Oh that one would hear me! Behold, my desire is, that the Almighty would answer me, and that mine adversary had written a book."
Job 31:35 (KJV)

Commentary:

Job's lament is certainly an understandable one. Beset by problems and overwhelming trouble from an unseen and unknown adversary, he cries out for a way to understand why and how these problems are being visited upon him.

Our spiritual adversary is both wise and crafty. He has not written a book and has no plans to reveal himself or his methods. He requires secrecy to accomplish his only goals which, according to John 10:10, are to "steal, kill, and destroy." He wants this world to be ignorant of him because it makes his deceptions harder to detect. That is why the greatest trick he could ever pull is to convince people he does not exist.

His desire for secrecy was thwarted because Jesus Christ came to open our eyes spiritually and show us the unseen spiritual warfare which rages all around us. We need not be ignorant of our spiritual enemy and his methods or devices because, even though he has not written a book, our God had one written for us. It contains information on how to become spiritually aware of the devil and his lies. Not only do we know he exists, thanks to God and His son, Jesus Christ, we know how to beat him.

Questions to consider while watching the film:

1. It has been said that knowledge is power. Why is this true and how does it apply to our spiritual lives?

2. How can we defend ourselves from an unseen opponent? How do we know if and when we are being deceived by our spiritual enemies?

Volunteers

on

Giving

Film: Volunteers (1985)
Directed by: Nicholas Meyer
Written by: David Isaacs, Ken Levine
U.S. Distributor: TriStar Pictures
Starring: Tom Hanks, John Candy, Rita Wilson
Rated: R

About the film:

A spoiled, rich ne'er-do-well runs up a huge debt which his tycoon father refuses to pay. In order to escape from his debtors, he enlists in the Peace Corps and finds himself in Southeast Asia where he is supposed to help the villagers build a bridge.

Movie Quote:

"It's not that I can't help these people. It's just I don't want to."
Lawrence Bourne III (Tom Hanks) in Volunteers (1985)

Bible Quote:

"Yet he did not waver through unbelief regarding the promise of God, but was strengthened in his faith and gave glory to God, being fully persuaded that God had power to do what He had promised."
Romans 4:20-21 (NIV)

Commentary:

At the beginning of the film, the central character of "Volunteers" is not a sterling example of altruism. And yet, if we are to be honest with ourselves, can any of us say that a similar sentiment to the one Bourne expresses has never entered our minds? Being of the flesh, we can sometimes get selfish with our time and energy by withholding our help from those in need.

Thankfully, we have a God who is better than man. His ability always equals His willingness. God does not withhold anything from us. If, in His Word, He has stated that something is available to us then we can know beyond any doubt that He is willing to give it to us. It does not matter what the promise is. Whether it is eternal life, health, prosperity, peace or happiness, once the promise is made, He backs it up with action.

The key to life is, and always has been, found in the principle of believing. It is a universal law that God has woven into all of His creation. As we believe, without doubting, we shall receive as long as the object of our desire does not contradict the stated will of God. If we want to receive blessings from God, the first step is to believe that He wants to give them to us.

Questions to consider while watching the film:

1. Positive thinking is something that is taught in secular self-help books. From a spiritual perspective, why does positive thinking work?

2. What changes in Bourne as a result of his experiences? What causes him to mature in his thinking and attitude?

Waking Life
on
Truth

Film: Waking Life (2001)
Directed by: Richard Linklater
Written by: Richard Linklater
U.S. Distributor: Fox Searchlight Pictures
Starring: Wiley Wiggins, Ethan Hawke, Julie Delpy
Rated: R

About the film:
An animated film follows a man in a dreamlike state. He meets a number of individuals who express their thoughts and opinions on a myriad of philosophical topics such as the meaning of life, death, and perception.

Movie Quote:
"The truth is out there in front of you, but they lay out this buffet of lies."
Man in Car (Alex Jones) in Waking Life (2001)

Bible Quote:
"And even if our gospel is veiled, it is veiled to those who are perishing. The god of this age has blinded the minds of unbelievers, so that they cannot see the light of the gospel of the glory of Christ, who is the image of God."
2 Corinthians 4:3-4 (NIV)

Commentary:

There is a truth that exists in this world. It is so strong and pure that no lie could ever stand against it. Our spiritual enemy knows this and so he does not present us with a "choose me or Him" ultimatum. He knows he would lose that gambit. Instead he relies on a complex ruse designed to confuse us.

The ploy our adversary takes can best be described as a spiritual "Where's Waldo" puzzle. The difficulty in "finding" Waldo in these puzzles comes from the abundant buffet of activity that fills the rest of the scene. There is only one Waldo, but there are hundreds of other images that distract us and keep us from seeing him. The point is that the devil does not care what we believe as long as it is not the truth. It is only the truth that can defeat him so it is the truth he must try to keep from us.

We must condition ourselves to focus on finding God's truth. It is the one truth set amid an ocean of lies. We need not be blinded or distracted from the truth God wants us to know. Finding it, like finding Waldo, can sometimes be difficult. But it is not impossible. It simply takes a concentrated effort, perseverance, and the ability to recognize it when you see it.

Questions to consider while watching the film:

1. The best lies are the ones which most closely resemble the truth. In what ways has our spiritual adversary used this reality to deceive people?

2. What enables us to discern between the truth and all the lies that contradict it? How do we keep our minds from being blinded?

A Walk to Remember
on
Plans

Film: A Walk to Remember (2002)
Directed by: Adam Shankman
Written by: Karen Janszen
U.S. Distributor: Warner Brothers
Starring: Shane West, Mandy Moore, Peter Coyote,
Rated: PG

About the film:

When bad boy Landon Carter gets into trouble, he is
sentenced to do community service which puts him in
close proximity to good girl Jaime Sullivan. Her faith and
his growing love for her cause him to reconsider what he
is doing with his life. Her influence changes him in
remarkable ways.

Movie Quote:

"Maybe God has a bigger plan for me than I had for
myself."

Jaime (Mandy Moore) in A Walk to Remember (2003)

Bible Quote:

"However, as it is written: 'No eye has seen, no ear has
heard, no mind has conceived what God has prepared for
those who love Him.'"

1 Corinthians 2:9 (NIV)

Commentary:

Jaime's faith is commendable and her understanding of God's love for her is inspiring. She may not fully comprehend what the future holds for her but she can trust in the One who does know. Whenever we can do that, our futures seem boundless.

It does not matter how grand a plan we might make for ourselves or how elaborate a dream we may be pursuing. God's ways and thoughts are infinitely larger. When we trust in Him to direct our steps, He will lead us to heights and places unimaginable.

It takes a certain amount of courage to walk down a path without knowing exactly where it might lead. But as we learn to trust in the one leading us down the path, we can venture on filled with great anticipation.

As we determine to follow God's will in our lives, setting aside our own doubts, fears, and selfish ambitions, we too shall see God's promises come to pass. And when God's promises eventually come to fruition, as they must always do, they will far exceed anything that we could ask or think for ourselves.

Questions to consider while watching the film:

1. Who has helped to shape you to become the person you are? Who has inspired you and why?

2. The way we live life is described in the Bible as a "walk." What are the characteristics of a walk and how do they parallel with the way we should approach life? What constitutes a "walk to remember"?

X-Men
on
Fear

Film: X-Men (2000)
Directed by: Bryan Singer
Written by: David Hayter
U.S. Distributor: 20th Century Fox
Starring: Hugh Jackman, Patrick Stewart
Rated: PG-13

About the film:
Believing that mankind would more readily accept mutant rights if everyone evolved at the same rate, Magneto builds a machine to expedite the mutation process in all of humanity. A small band of mutant superheroes led by Professor X sets out to stop him before he reshapes the world in his own image.

Movie Quote:
"Mankind has always feared what it doesn't understand."
Magneto (Ian McKellen) in X-Men (2000)

Bible Quote:
"He said to his disciples, 'Why are you so afraid? Do you still have no faith?'"
Mark 4:40 (NIV)

MICHAEL ELLIOTT

Commentary:

Magneto may be misguided in his actions but he is
cognizant of an important truth. Man does tend to fear
the unknown.

If fear is born of ignorance, the solution to fear is
obvious. Knowledge, which leads to understanding,
empowers us. It fuels us with the strength and confidence
we need to prevail over the temptation to fear.

There is no greater knowledge available to acquire
than the knowledge of God. The more we know of Him,
His love for us, and His desire for our lives, the less
reason we will have to fear.

In the quoted scripture, the word "faith" can also be
translated to read "believing." We can grow fearful when
we fail to believe God's promises. And we cannot truly
believe what we do not understand. To strengthen our
believing requires that we grow in our knowledge of
God's Word.

"Consequently, faith comes from hearing the
message, and the message is heard through the word of
Christ." Romans 10:17 (NIV)

Questions to consider while watching the film:

1. What are some examples where God must
   instruct someone to "fear not" or "have no fear"
   before He can tell them what they need to hear?

2. Scripture says that the antidote to fear is love.
   Why is that true?

You Again
on
Attitude

Film: You Again (2010)
Directed by: Andy Fickman
Written by: Moe Jelline
U.S. Distributor: Touchstone Pictures
Starring: Kristen Bell, Odette Annable
Rated: PG

About the film:
A young public relations executive learns that the "mean girl" from high school, who made her teenaged life a living hell, is engaged to her brother. What is a girl to do? She cannot go to her mother for advice because mom is dealing with a different crisis. Mom and the new bride-to-be's aunt have a history of their own.

Movie Quote:
"You can't control the things that happen to you but you can control how you react to them."
Marni (Kristen Bell) in You Again (2010)

Bible Quote:
"See that none render evil for evil unto any man; but ever follow that which is good, both among yourselves, and to all men."
1 Thessalonians 5:15 (KJV)

Commentary:

For many people, "turning the other cheek" is easier said than done. However, we see from the Bible that it is possible. And more than possible, it is encouraged. The benefits that come to us when we follow God's exhortations will so greatly outweigh the outcome of any alternative course of action that there really is no choice at all.

Granted, life is difficult at times. Few of us will get through it completely unscathed. We will have bad times; we will experience unpleasant events; we will find ourselves in unjust situations. But nothing we face need dictate to us how we are to respond. We can operate on a higher plane.

God has given us, through the incredible design of the human body, the ability to control our minds. By controlling our minds, we have control over our thoughts, our actions, and even the responses we choose during negative situations.

God certainly does not want us to be life-long victims, subject to the abuse of everyone else. But neither does He want us to use unjust abuse as an excuse to act in opposition to all He teaches us. It remains our choice, of course. But He has clearly pointed us in the direction He would desire us to go.

Questions to consider while watching the film:

1. How does forgiveness figure into the film's story? Who shows the most forgiveness?

2. What is the best answer to a bullying situation? What would be the Christian response?

Zero Effect
on
Research

Film: Zero Effect (1998)
Directed by: Jake Kasdan
Written by: Jake Kasdan
U.S. Distributor: Columbia Pictures
Starring: Bill Pulman, Ben Stiller, Ryan O'Neal
Rated: R

About the film:
Daryl Zero is the world's greatest detective, able to piece together isolated fragments of clues in order to solve his case. His only problem is that he is so socially inept he requires the use of a front man in order to interact with those who hire him.

Movie Quote:
"For every event, there is a cause and effect. For every crime - a motive; and for every motive - a passion. The art of research is the ability to look at the details and see the passion."
Daryl Zero (Bill Pullman) in Zero Effect (1998)

Bible Quote:
"Study to show thyself approved unto God, a workman that needeth not to be ashamed, rightly dividing the word of truth."
2 Timothy 2:15 (KJV)

Commentary:

Zero's methodology of criminal research actually mirrors a key principle to biblical study. Scripture says that God has given us all things pertaining to life and godliness. God's Word allows us the opportunity to grow closer to Him because He reveals Himself to us through His Word. But it requires the ability to see His truth while reading His Word.

"Rightly dividing" the Bible requires diligence, commitment, perseverance, and faithfulness. Above all, it requires a considerable amount of meekness as we must be willing to research the Word without forcing our own preconceived and prejudicial ideas into what we read. We must learn to read the Word instead of reading into the Word. To rightly divide means to "make a straight cut." There is only one interpretation that has significance or power and that is God's interpretation.

The benefits of honestly "working the Word" are innumerable. As we closely examine all the details which God has woven into His Word and see how they fit so perfectly together, we can understand more clearly His divine nature which includes the passionate and unconditional love He has for us.

Questions to consider while watching the film:

1. If there is one way to "rightly divide" the Bible, why is there so much doctrinal disagreement between the various Christian denominations?

2. If everything in the Bible was given to us by a perfect and infallible God, why do there seem to be discrepancies in the text? What are we to do as "workmen" when we come across an apparent discrepancy?

MOVIE INDEX

Adjustment Bureau, The 5
Air Force One 7
Alice in Wonderland 9
All the King's Men 11
American Splendor 13
Amistad 15
Angels & Demons 17
Apollo 13 19
Apostle, The 21
Apt Pupil 23
Barbershop 25
Being There 27
Cape Fear 29
Chariots of Fire 31
City of Angels 33
Clean and Sober 35
Contact 37
Contender, The 39
Crimson Tide 41
Crouching Tiger, Hidden
Dragon 43
Deconstructing Harry 45
Dogma 47
Don Juan de Marco 49
Doubt 51
Emperor's Club, The 53
Enemy at the Gates 55
Evan Almighty 57
Facing the Giants 59
Fight Club 61
First Knight 63
Fisher King, The 65
Fly Away Home 67
Frost/Nixon 69
Grand Canyon 71
Great Buck Howard, The 73
Great Debaters, The 75
Green Mile, The 77
Hellboy 79
High Fidelity 81
Hitch 83
Independence Day 85
Kate and Leopold 87
King's Speech, The 89
Kite Runner, The 91
Knight's Tale, A 93
Knowing 95
Ladyhawke 97
Lean on Me 99
Liar, Liar 101
Man in the Iron Mask, The 103
Matrix, The 105

Matrix Reloaded, The 107
Mississippi Burning 109
Moonstruck 111
Mr. Deeds 113
Natural, The 115
Nixon 117
Notebook, The 119
O Brother, Where Art Thou? .. 121
Once Upon a Time When
We Were Colored 123
Patch Adams 125
Preacher's Wife, The 127
Ratatouille 129
Razor's Edge, The 131
Rock Star 133
Rocky IV 135
Roxanne 137
Shadowlands 139
Shall We Dance? 141
Sicko 143
Solaris 145
Soloist, The 147
Source Code 149
Spider-man 151
Spy Game 153
Star Trek 155
Star Trek II 157
Star Trek VI 159
Star Wars 161
Star Wars Episode V 163
Star man 165
Sunshine (2007) 167
Sunshine (1999) 169
Talk Radio 171
Thirteen Conversations
About One Thing 173
Thirteen Days 175
Time Bandits 177
Tombstone 179
Top Gun 181
Toy Story 3 183
Troy 185
Tuck Everlasting 187
Ultimate Gift, The 189
Untouchables, The 191
Usual Suspects, The 193
Volunteers 195
Waking Life 197
Walk to Remember, A 199
X-Men 201
You Again 203
Zero Effect 205

TOPIC INDEX

Adversity 165
Anger 77
Appearances 163
Attitude 203
Behavior 83
Believing 33, 105, 127
Change 135, 137
Confidence 141
Contentment 89
Darkness 79
Death 145, 187
Debt 143
Decisions 81, 129
Devil 193
Diligence 133
Discipline 99
Doubt 51
Dual Citizenship 155
Ego 169
Envy 55
Evil 177
Failure 19
Faithfulness 43, 183
Fear 201
Fools 113
Free Will 5
Freedom 15
Gifts 23
Giving 195
God 161
God's Word 71
Growth 27
Habits 35
Hatred 109
Heaven 21
Hope 93
Human Weakness 97
Ignorance 41
Illusions 73
Image of God 65
Impossibilities 59
Integrity 9
Jesus Christ 131
Knowledge 11, 137
Leaders 103
Light 167
Limitations 13
Logic 121, 159
Longevity 157
Love 49, 119

Loyalty 147
Luck 173
Lying 91, 101
Martyrdom 47
Meekness 39
Men of Good Will 175
Natural Abilities 115
Now 75
Past 29
Peace 7
Perseverance 31, 191
Plans 199
Possessions 61
Prayer 57, 139
Preparation 153
Problem Solving 125
Promises 67
Prophecy 95
Purpose 37, 69, 107
Research 205
Resentment 117
Responsibility 151
Science 17
Self-Discipline 189
Self-Improvement 181
Stars 179
Study 123
Stupidity 53
Time 149
Tradition 45
Truth 197
Unity 85
Wants 87
War 185
Wealth 25
Wisdom 63
Women 111
Words 171

SCRIPTURE INDEX

GENESIS
1:27 .... 65, 66
2:18 112

NUMBERS
23:19 101

DEUTERONOMY
5:21 55
30:11 137
31:8 161

JOSHUA
1:9 183

2 SAMUEL
22:34 141

JOB
21:34 91
31:35 193

PSALMS
8:3 179
8:4 179
84:10 21
100:3 34
103:13 97
103:14 97
106:23 175
111:10 159

PROVERBS
1:7 53
2:3 11
2:4 11
2:5 11
3:5 .... 13, 115
3:6 13
12:18 172
13:4 133
13:7 25
14:30 56
15:1 77
22:7 143
25:28 99
28:20 43
28:26 121

ECCLESIASTES
5:4 67
5:5 67
12:13 37

ISAIAH
45:7 177

MATTHEW
7:14 131
12:36 68
13 28
14:31 51
15:3 45
16:26 118
24:37 153

MARK
4 28
4:40 201
9:23 105
11:24 140
12:30 108

LUKE
8 28
9:5 117
12:15 61
12:48 151
14:11 159
16:17 19
18:27 59

JOHN
1:1 160
1:5 167
3:6 155
4:24 .... 66, 136
8:32 .... 92, 102
10:10 194
14:6 132
14:27 7

ACTS
3:19 135

ROMANS
3:3 33
3:4 33
3:31 17

ROMANS (continued)
4:19 125
4:20 125,195
4:21 195
6:9 145
8:37 165,166
10:9 22,136,154
10:10 22,136,154
10:17 202
12:21 178
12:6 23
12:7 23
13:11 75

1 CORINTHIANS
2:9 199
11:7 111
11:8 111
12:7 95
13:13 49
14:3 96
15:33 .... 24, 113

2 CORINTHIANS
4:3 197
4:4 197
5:7 127
6:14 79
9:6 158
9:8 57

GALATIANS
1:10 9
5:1 5

EPHESIANS
1:11 107
2:1 15
2:2 15
2:12 136
3:4 58,123
3:20 87
4:2 86
4:3 86
4:14 73
4:30 47
5 112
5:16 149
6:2 158
6:3 158

PHILIPPIANS
2:2 85
3:13 29
3:14 29
3:20 156

PHILIPPIANS (continued)
4:11 90
4:19 58

COLOSSIANS
2:6 27
2:7 27
3:9 35
3:10 35

1 THESSALONIANS
1:5 83
4:1 10
5:5 203

1 TIMOTHY
6:6 89
6:7 89
6:8 89
6:12 192

2 TIMOTHY
2:15 203
4:7 191

TITUS
1:2 102

HEBREWS
2:14 187
2:15 187
6:19 93
12:1 31
12:2 31
12:11 189

JAMES
1:5 63
1:6 52
1:7 52
1:8 .... 52, 81
1:23 181
1:24 181
1:25 173
3:7 171
3:8 171
3:13 39
4:1 185
4:14 69
5:16 139

1 PETER
2:15 41
2:24 58

2 PETER
1:3 71

1 JOHN
2:11 109
4:4 163
4:11 119
4:19 38

3 JOHN
1:2 157
1:4 178

REVELATION
2:10 147
3:15 129
17:14 103

www.ingramcontent.com/pod-product-compliance
Lightning Source LLC
Chambersburg PA
CBHW031316040426
42443CB00005B/96